T0156997

FORTY DAYS
DAYS
with
RUTH

CAROL WELTY ROPER

Order this book online at www.trafford.com
or email orders@trafford.com

Most Trafford titles are also available at major online book retailers.

© Copyright 2018 Carol Welty Roper.
All rights reserved. No part of this publication may be reproduced, stored in a retrieval
system, or transmitted, in any form or by any means, electronic, mechanical, photocopying,
recording, or otherwise, without the written prior permission of the author.

Print information available on the last page.

ISBN: 978-1-4907-8957-6 (sc)
ISBN: 978-1-4907-8958-3 (hc)
ISBN: 978-1-4907-8959-0 (e)

Library of Congress Control Number: 2018907209

Because of the dynamic nature of the Internet, any web addresses or links contained in
this book may have changed since publication and may no longer be valid. The views
expressed in this work are solely those of the author and do not necessarily reflect the
views of the publisher, and the publisher hereby disclaims any responsibility for them.

Any people depicted in stock imagery provided by Getty Images are models,
and such images are being used for illustrative purposes only.
Certain stock imagery © Getty Images.

Trafford rev. 06/26/2018

 www.trafford.com

North America & international
toll-free: 1 888 232 4444 (USA & Canada)
fax: 812 355 4082

CONTENTS

PREFACE.. vii
ACKNOWLEDGMENTS.. ix
CHARACTER ANALYSIS xi

Chapter 1   SORRY HONEY, I HAVE TO GO.............................. 1
Chapter 2   THE STUFF THAT MAKES DREAMS 10
Chapter 3   EVERYTHING HAS TO EAT 16
Chapter 4   PREPARE FOR BATTLE.................................... 26
Chapter 5   BE SEEING YOU, IF ONLY IN MY DREAMS.......... 38
Chapter 6   SURVIVING OR THRIVING?.............................. 44
Chapter 7   RUTH REDEFINED 54
Chapter 8   LIVING IN A NEW REVELATION 61
Chapter 9   LIVING LIFE AS A TRUE ADVENTURE 65

RECIPES FOUND IN THE STORY FORTY DAYS WITH
RUTH 73

PREFACE

In August of 2009, I flew from my home in Alaska to my birth home in Oklahoma. I drove from the Oklahoma City airport to the town of Duncan and then on to Ryan, Oklahoma to visit the grave site of my grandmother; Ruth Stewart Welty. When I stepped out of my rental car, I was greeted with a gust of wind that came up suddenly and took my breath away. As I looked in the direction of the Red River, the land and foliage were the greenest I had ever seen during an Oklahoma summer. I returned to my car and traveled down the dirt road to the place where Ruth and Riley first lived in a dugout and later built a farm house. It was not exactly how I remembered it. There were more trees than when I was growing up, however when my feet touched the red dirt and I walked over to the wild plum thicket and then looked over to the creek full of water, everything was exactly as I remembered. I looked to the sky, and there riding the thermals was a red-tailed hawk. We shared a moment and then I left.

As I drove back to Duncan that afternoon, I turned on the radio to the station that played tear-jerking country Western songs. With all the windows rolled down, I felt the wind on my face and it blowing my hair. I sang out as loud as I could. I needed that wind so I could smell those earthy smells of growing blowing things. I needed the sights and smells to remember.

Clouds were forming in the southwest, hiding the sun. Those dark clouds couldn't contain the sun rays that escaped and cascaded down upon the lush green pasture land dotted with Angus and Polled Hereford cattle. Cicadas sang out from the pecan trees and muffled the music coming from the radio. A truck stop promised on its sign a cold drink was waiting for me, so I took a minute to stop for one. I was back in Oklahoma and I felt blessed. It was at that moment I knew I needed to tell my grandmother's story that Riley Welty, my papaw, told me years ago over breakfast one summer morning. The rest of the bits and pieces of this tale is pure inspiration.

I hope *Forty Days with Ruth* will bless you in some way. I dedicate this novel to Ruth Stewart Welty and to her great-great granddaughter, Shelby Rae Beuch.

ACKNOWLEDGMENTS

I wish to acknowledge and give my gratitude to my Heavenly Father for giving me a brave and God-fearing heritage. With humble gratitude I thank the LORD for inspiring me to write and share some of my family's stories. The help I received from friends and family is greatly appreciated. My husband, Philip Roper, is a great encourager. Dr. Kim Kjaersgaard graciously edited and advised me on the manuscript. Thank you.

Jennifer Bowers, my daughter, was my first-read and demanded I write more than what appeared on the first draft. Thanks for cheering me on. Very special thanks to Kim LeGay, who prayed for me years ago to be courageous and rely on the Holy Spirit for guidance in this creative process. I am happy for the support of my Church family and my sisters in Christ who call me to come out and play and be the woman God created me to be. Thank you Kim Armstrong, Amanda Clifford, Kam Dodson, Lelani Dodson, Elisha Heagy, Gina Jones, Janet Kurkendyll, Hazel "Gizzy" Kruse, Gerry Lange, Ruth McClain, Lucia Nanez, Julie Pollard, Mary Remole, and Shelly Sparks.

FORTY DAYS WITH RUTH: CHARACTER ANALYSIS

RUTH STEWART WELTY:

Ruth, a young Texan woman born to Scottish immigrants, has eloped with Riley Earl Welty. They barely know one another and have run away across the Red River to the Oklahoma Territory.

Forty Days with Ruth is a coming-of-age story. Ruth is no longer a child but not yet an adult. Her unquestioned perception of life is what she has been told to her by family and friends.

Ruth stands four feet eleven inches tall, and she weighs ninety pounds. Her hair is long, thin and auburn, framing brown eyes and a lightly freckled face. Her personality is melancholy, moody and shy. She loves all animals except for snakes. Ruth has a beautiful singing voice, but she only sings whenever she is out of the earshot of others. Highly imaginative, she has a great capacity to daydream. Naturally spiritual, she has an intimate relationship with all lifeforms but not so much with other humans. Her paternal grandmother, Granny Stewart, claims Ruth has the gift of sight, translated as a keen sensitivity to the moving of the Holy Spirit.

Romance, fun, adventure and a man who will love her just as she is are all she dreams about in life. She desires to be happy and defines happiness as being close to God, becoming a loving wife and mother, then making a safe and beautiful home for her family. This dream home must be on land she can care for, and the land's resources will gift her and her family with food, shelter, safety and enjoyment. Her hope is to have enough food for her family and enough to share with her neighbors. All these things, she believes, will allow her to live in harmony with the land and with all who view the land as a gift from God.

The ideal man who will become her husband and the father of her children will be God-fearing, honest, fun and generous. It wouldn't hurt her feelings if he was also handsome. But he must love horses and children,and be willing to dance.

Ruth has a deep desire to have a garden similar to the one Granny Stewart planted and harvested each year. Ruth wants one that will have a variety of flowers, vegetables and medicinal plants. Granny taught her that the Bible records in the beginning life started in a garden. In her garden she longs to sing the bees and butterflies to her plants so they will move among the blooms in the sun and perform their pollination dance.

RILEY EARL WELTY:

Riley Earl Welty, a young man born to Swiss immigrants, left his home in Texas to work for hire. His only work experience has been on farms and ranches. Blessed to get a job from a rancher who needs some cowboys, he hires on to drive a herd of long horned steers from South Texas all the way to Kansas. With the job completed and money in his pocket, he is headed back to his home in Texas.

Riley is handsome, and he knows it. He also has an eye for pretty girls. His lack of social skills result in mostly looking without touching. He's generally carefree, happy to be alive. Riley would be considered, by his family, more of an impulsive thinker than a logical thinker. He wants what he believes everyone wants: some land to call his own, a woman who will love and care for him; maybe some children, maybe some livestock. He is unquestionably confident God will provide, because that is what God does. Riley knows he will live a long life and find happiness along the way. He knows this because his father accomplished neither, and it is Riley's destiny to live a better life than his father.

Standing five feet and four inches tall in his stocking feet and weighing a hundred thirty pounds soaking wet, he is a proud, stout, blue-eyed blonde made of solid muscle and bone. He has a taste for chewing tobacco and, occasionally, a cigar. He doesn't drink alcohol very often, however he will never pass up a drink if someone's buying. This young man loves to eat and can go to sleep at the drop of a hat. In jest, he likes to say he will be willing to drop the hat. Manual labor fills up the rest of his day. His work pace is a bit slower that most others, although he does stick with it until the job is completed. Riley just naturally likes to play and tease. Most of Riley's friends believed that while he was growing up, he didn't take life seriously.

Riley, known by his friends as, Rye, has faith in the Creator of the Universe. He reasoned things were just as they are; he didn't much care why.

GRANNY STEWART:

Granny Stewart never lived to see Ruth married. Granny just didn't wake up one morning. The family buried her next to her husband in the family plot under the large oak tree in the knoll behind the ranch house. Next to her beloved husband William Stewart, they placed a stone in her name: Sara Cockburn Steward. Willy, as she called him, died two years after their granddaughter Ruth was born. Sally, as Willly called his wife, went to live with their son, John, and his family. William didn't want his wife to live alone, so it was determined long before his death that Sally Stewart, known to all as Granny, would live with his family for the rest of her life.

Granny was a spry small woman with boundless energy. She was short yet stout, light in weight and able to work three grown men into the ground. Those that knew her said she was a force to be reckoned with, and yet they all agreed, Granny was as good as they come. Even so, the woman was either on or off; meaning, awake or sound asleep. Every day she rose in the dark of the morning and had breakfast cooked within the hour. Breakfast didn't vary much. It was always some variation of biscuits, bannock, pancakes or fruited scones, meat, eggs and porridge with plenty of freshly churned butter and cool buttermilk, homemade fruit syrup and jam. Everyone had to have their daily dose of castor oil and apple cider vinegar, and this duty she made sure of by personally doling it out to the family before they sat down at the table.

Lunch and dinner was always decided before breakfast was finished and preparation was started before the breakfast dishes were washed and put away. Soups and stews were the quickest fare during the weekdays while there was time-consuming chores to be done, such as washing, pressing, baking, gardening, canning, sewing, mending, knitting, housekeeping, letter writing, tending to the chickens and gathering the eggs, butter-churning, farmer-cheese-making and a slew of other chores. On Saturday, much of the day was spent preparing for a big Sunday dinner. A pie or cake was baked, a fat chicken was plucked and dressed, or else, a cured ham was put to soak. Sunday and holidays were the only times the fine dishes were used, and many of them were fine treasures brought to Texas all the way from Scotland. Saturday evening each family member took turns taking a bath and making sure their Sunday clothes were cleaned and pressed and shoes polished. The women folk were privileged to use some of Granny's rose water and glycerin soap to wash their hair; a treat because the fragrance would linger for a couple of days.

Sundays, while the family was dressing, the horse was hitched up to the buggy, and Bibles were fetched; Granny was dishing up porridge for a quick breakfast before Church services. Some friends from Church and the pastor and his wife were invited to share dinner, to eat and visit, play games and enjoy one another during the Sabbath rest. After the company left, everyone took a nap while Granny washed and carefully put away the fine dinnerware. The children were made to help during the rest of the week, but Granny insisted she would be the only one to clean up after Sunday dinner so the fine dishes were handled with care.

Granny Stewart had no trouble working and talking a mile a minute at the same time. People could easily observe this behavior and mistakenly think she was talking to herself until they listened closely to hear she was praying or softly singing a hymn. Every day of the year, an hour after supper was time for scripture reading. All of her children and grandchildren learned to read from the scriptures with the help of the grownups. This was also time for family discussion that involved the farm business, and no one was excused from the table. Well, one may be excused if a calf or foal was being born and needed tending, or, once in a long while, when a misbehaving child needed an attitude adjustment administered to the seat of their pants.

Bedtime was always Ruth's favorite time with Granny Stewart because this was when she had her all to herself. Granny would tell her stories that were not in books. Some of these stories were true, and some were not. Ruth never seemed to know which was which, but didn't mind; she loved them all.

ARENUMI:

Arenumi was from the Comanche tribe. Her most notable quality was her white well-aligned teeth that were framed by lovely full lips. She smiled easily at those she knew. Neither eyes nor teeth were shown to strangers. Her blue-black hair was worn either cascading down her back or plaited tightly into two thick braids. Her ageless face was soft and smooth with taut skin void of blemishes or scars. The loose clothing she wore, made from feed-sack cotton, couldn't conceal her curvaceous figure. Every part of her appearance revealed a beautiful specimen of womanhood, strong and healthy, and her spirit a pleasing testament of human kindness. Arenumi's countenance was not obviously marred by her difficult and troubled past. In spite of that, her eyes drew a person to see her hope, contentment, with a spark of mirth and mischief. This woman knew things and was willing to teach, if a person was willing to learn.

JOHN STEWART:

John Stewart, the father of Ruth, was born in a small village near Edinburgh, Scotland. He was an infant when his family settled in Northwestern Texas, near a place named Possum Kingdom. He married seventeen-year-old Molly MacCleod, a Scottish immigrant.

John, a mountain of muscle, sinew and bone, possessed a sterling reputation for strength and endurance as a youth participating in the annual Caledonia Heavy Event Games. He was champion three years in a row in caber-tree-trunk toss and stone putting. John was attending one of these festivities when he caught the heart of his true love Molly. They courted the customary year and were married with a wedding that lasted three days.

He loved carrying Molly around since she was a wee slip of a girl. She would squeal and make a fuss, but everyone knew she loved to play; and more than that, she loved the big strong brute of a man who planted roses for her just because she once told him she fancied them.

Their firstborn James was strong and powerful, a somewhat smaller version of his father. Both shared a quick temper and a tendency to hold a grudge. To balance out this negative trait, they both shared a good humor and loved a clever story or a joke now and then. Smart, hardworking, and loyal were the characteristics that drew others to remain their friends for life.

However, John was tougher physically and would fight bare-fisted if anyone needed a whipping. He was equally as good with a gun. He showed no tolerance for injustice and didn't condone hangings or prejudice toward Indians, immigrants, Mexicans, ex-slaves, or Jews. He took pride in being a Texan. There was land a plenty for any God-fearing people who wanted to work to make a living and raise wholesome families.

He was tough yet tender. He adored his women: mother, wife and daughter. There would be hell to pay if anyone hurt them or even was discourteous to one of them. Although his love was undeniable, equality between the sexes seemed too foreign of a concept for him to entertain.

One group of people was the exception to the rule in his life. John Stewart couldn't abide the group who drove long-horned steers from South Texas up to the rails in Kansas. They were transient, dirty low-life monsters who worked good horses to death, drove diseased cattle that spread their sickness to farmer's dairy cows and used up the clean water in the streams so others had to find water elsewhere. This group of hoodlums drank cheap whiskey and would whore around every town they passed through. Many couldn't read and most displayed no manners. They were horrid and despicable. This group were given the name cowboys. Hum, cowboys was an appropriate name, in John's opinion, because they were immature and reckless, not worthy of being called men.

MOLLY MACCLEOD STEWART:

Molly MacCLeod moved from the misty heather-covered highlands of Scotland to the hot bluebell-covered plains of Texas. Her family settled among her clan near a small town named Bowie. In Scotland, everyone was poor. She knew some who died from sickness brought on just because they didn't have enough to eat. Molly had never owned shoes until she came to Texas and her aunt Ruth Ann had given her a new pair of shoes and some socks. She was so happy because this meant she was rich.

Molly was the sixth daughter of nine children. Her mama had one child every year for ten straight years, and thanks to the good Lord, only one died in childhood.

Life in Texas was so much better now that they had some land of their own to farm. They raised cattle, mostly dairy cattle and hogs, chickens, goats and a few turkeys.

From dawn until well into the night, Molly grew up helping her family with chores. At age six, Molly was already helping her sisters cook, wash the dishes, press the clean laundry, weed the garden, gather eggs and clean out the stalls in the barn. As she grew, she would go with her mother and sisters to quilting bees and learn other sewing projects. She loved sewing and was very gifted with a needle and thread. Frugality grew out of living without many resources, so every scrap of cloth and every crumb of bread was used. And Heaven forbid, if any were wasted, it was treated as a severe punishable sin.

Molly learned very early that the most important things were to give your best to the Lord and to remain steadfast and loyal to your family. Life was uncomplicated; a person was either right or wrong. If her pa said it was so, then it was right. But anything that strayed from what he said was, by all means, wrong.

Back in Scotland, people stayed close to their clan and didn't venture out to mingle among other clans- that is, the women folk didn't. Her pa said that Texas was his clan's starting-over place, and they would be neighborly to some other Scots who had settled nearby them. So from time to time, they would all get together; pull out their fiddles, drums and pipes and have themselves good fun. Everyone would bring food and some homemade liquor; sing, dance and party until the moon moved overhead in the sky. Then they would load the families up in their wagons and go back to their farms because cows would need to be milked early in the morning.

These gatherings were as far as Molly had ever been from her home in Texas until she was sixteen years old. For her birthday, her pa thought she was mostly a full grown woman, and she and her sisters and brothers could go to the annual Caledonia Heavy Event Games. It was at this event Molly met John. They were smitten with each other. Then John and his parents called on Molly's parents. An agreement granted John permission to court Molly.

They married and had a son and a daughter. Life was good. Everyone had plenty to eat and enough to share. They raised good Morgan horses and made a decent living selling their horses to the army post at Ft. Sill.

Life was good until a major change happened in Molly's life. Molly's widowed mother-in-law moved to live with their family.

Molly MacCleod Stewart lived in the shadow of her mother-in-law Granny Stewart. Granny was kind and never seemed cross or ill-tempered at anything. Everything she did, she told people, she did it unto the Lord. So, of course, everything she did was excellent-that was the problem.

SADIE:

Sadie is Ruth's wonderful Morgan horse, friend, companion and partner in secrets.

BUSTER:

Buster is the Stewart family's cow dog, protector and partner in secrets also.

HELPER:

She is the red tailed hawk who helped Ruth survive on the prairie.

MR. LIZARD:

He is Ruth's horned lizard pet, and he keeps her living area free from ants and other vermin.

CHAPTER 1

SORRY HONEY, I HAVE TO GO

Riley aimed his Winchester, then slowly squeezed the trigger. A deafening shot rang out, bullet hitting the target. The tall jack rabbit fell out of sight, flushing out three more rabbits. A second shot took down a smaller one. Ruth slowly unplugged her fingers from her ears. The acrid smell of gun smoke invaded Ruth's nose. With one hand she held the reins of Sadie, her nervous gun-shy horse; and with the other hand, she covered her nose as she sneezed. Ruth still had her eyes tightly shut, not wanting to watch and trying not to cry. She was glad for the meat but the tears were because all hope of going with Riley deer hunting died with those two jack rabbits whereas, Riley, could leave knowing Ruth had some food to last for a while.

Riley ran through the tall grass and fetched the fresh game.

"Looky here, Darlin'," he said with a big grin on his face as he held up the rabbits for her to admire. He halfway hopped and ran with excitement as he carried his prize to their sod house. Slowly she opened her eyes to a squint. Showing no enthusiasm she followed him to examine the fresh meat that would be part of her supper. Sadie stopped nibbling on the Johnson grass and followed her to the dugout.

Riley smiled a toothy grin at his new wife and handed her the fresh game. She took the rabbits but didn't return his smile as she handed him the reins of her Morgan horse. Riley wiped his hands on some tall grass, then turned to stroke Sadie to calm her. The horse avoided his touch by moving a few steps and gave Ruth a reluctant look. Riley missed their exchange as he busied himself finishing his preparation for the hunting trip. He bent over to cinch the saddle strap as he spoke.

"*This here game ought to feed ya for a day or two, 'til I get back with some deer or buffalo.*"

"*Oh please, Riley, take me with you. I can hunt too.*" Ruth whined. This was the umpteenth time she tried to get her way

Riley looked Ruth straight in the eye and his jolly demeanor changed to sober.

"*Darlin', I'll tell you one more time. Be reasonable about this. We only have one horse and one rifle. You don't have the clothes to go huntin' and there's a whole slew of other reasons why it'd be better for you to stay here. You got those rabbits to eat on until I can get us some real big game. Ruthy, you'll be just fine.*"

"*But how long will you be gone? I'm scared here without you. I'll miss you. What in the world will I do? We run out of food. It's too far into town for me to walk for supplies. You're taking the horse and leaving me the wagon. Oh, I wish I was home or at least not so far away from everybody!*" She tried to win him over by looking as pathetic as possible.

"*Ruth, don't start on me again, about wantin' to leave and go home. I thought we settled all that last night. You kissed me and told me you loved me and would never leave me. Did you mean it darlin'? I got to know that you'll be here when I get back. You knew when you run off with me that you would be leaving your ma and all your kin behind. Ain't I enough for ya?*"

"*Yes. I'm just talking crazy. I'm just worried.*" Her pout was not working to change his mind to see her way of thinking.

"*Well, don't worry. I promise I'll come back.*"

"*Riley remember that we need more than just meat. You got my list with you?*"

He pulled out the paper from his pocket, unfolded it, and read her the list she'd made for him.

"*I've got here some flour, lard, coffee, fat back, a few layin' hens and feed, some oats for the horse, some yarn and needles. I've got to get some meat to trade off so I can pay for what we need. Don't you realize I've got to go, and the sooner I leave, the sooner I'll be right back here lookin' after ya. You got to face up to the fact we're grown-up people now, and sometimes we've got to do hard thangs.*"

Still holding the rabbits, Ruth wiped the tears from her eyes with her free hand.

"*Sweet Ruth, stop cryin' and come give me a kiss before I go. Can I have a little smile from you also so I can take that with me to think on while I ride out?*"

"But Riley…Oh all right, *you make me want to be generous whenever you talk to me that way.*" She walked over and kissed him and held on until he pulled away.

"*I don't see no smilin' on them lips I just kissed.*" She gave him a faint smile.

"*That's my girl. You're my best girl ever and my only girl from now on. I'll come home with a big deer or maybe a buffalo, if there's any still left roamin' around. When I get back with the meat you'll be so doggone busy cleanin', butcherin', and cookin' you'll wish you had some time alone just for yourself. You've got the pistol and the extra bullets. I'm sure ya won't have any need to use it. I'm leaving it for your own safety. Don't go out to greet nobody if they happen this way unless the Lord leads ya to do so. You ain't alone. He's keepin' watch over ya. Ruth, believe me, don't ya?*"

"*I do. Oh, I'm acting like such a big baby. You go be that big hunter, and I'll stay behind keeping the home fire burning and that fire in my heart burning for you too. Get out of here, now.*" Her tough act quickly caved.

"*Sweetheart, you will be sure to be careful, won't you? You promise me right now, Riley Earl, to come back to me and don't be long doing it. You hear me?*"

He tipped his hat to his lady and mounted the horse in one movement.

"*So help me God, I love you, and I promise you right here and now that I'll come back to you and love ya the rest of my life.*" He looked up into the sky and then down into the teary eyes of his wife. He whispered so she wouldn't hear.

"*The Lord willing.*"

Ruth sighed in defeat, looked at Sadie's sad eyes and then to both of them she waved goodbye.

The southwest wind blew her hair out of its tight bun. Unaffected, she let her loose hair blow freely. She watched and waved until she couldn't see them anymore. That wind was so strong it finally broke the spell that had paralyzed her. Ruth turned away and reluctantly stepped inside the dugout. By now, Riley and Sadie were far out of sight, so she decided to focus on other duties instead of looking at an empty horizon. Hot tears ran through the silty red dust on her cheeks. Her lips had a salty grit when she licked them, and it collected on her tongue, forming a lump in her throat. Ruth's whole body felt miserable and totally alone. But then she remembered her husband's parting words.

3

"Lord Jesus, it's just you and me now. This must have been how you felt whenever you walked into the wilderness alone. I need your protection and your help. Please take care of Riley and let him have a successful hunt. You know how much we need some food. And please watch over Sadie. We need her more than ever. Thank you for the rabbits." She paused for what seemed a long while and let out a heavy sigh.

"And Lord, thank you for giving me Riley to love. Amen."

As she stood looking out the door, Ruth's thoughts traveled back to why she was now so far away from any living soul. Her parents had no doubt read her note she had left them after Riley and she had eloped. The same traveling revival preacher who led the Holy Spirit brush arbor meetings had hesitantly agreed to marry them. Ruth's pa, no doubt, had mounted up with some of his neighbors to help search for Riley and her. Pa's temper ran hot if anyone disobeyed him. At the time when she eloped and ran away, she feared for Riley's life, but Ruth was confident no one would ever be able to find her. What a perfect hiding place across the Red River, in the territory where no white people lived. Who would think to go there to find them? At this minute, she hoped someone would. The thought actually made her bristle. Ruth quickly changed her mind. Now she didn't care if she ever was found, at least not by her family. Angry thoughts were forming into one big grudge. Ruth spoke to the wind as if it would carry her message back to her parent's ears.

"Why don't you like Riley? He's a good man, fun-loving, hard-working. He just needs some land to work. We won't always be poor. No, you didn't even try to get to know him. He was no better than manure on your shoe. It was downright shameful the way you both treated him when I introduced him to our neighbors at our church arbor meeting. When it came time to auction the pies for the missionary fund-raiser, Riley was the highest bidder for my pie. He sat right down and ate the whole pie. That was the pie that you, Ma, said was too ugly to slop to the hogs!" Her hands were rolled into tight fists as angry tears followed those sad tears shed for Riley's leaving.

"Ma, that was a hateful thing to say to me. I have you know, Riley told me he thought it was delicious. He likes me, Ma. He says I'm pretty, and he don't care who hears it. No, you're right, he ain't as big and strong as Pa. I like him just the way he is. I love him, and he loves me. We are happy together. You'll see. We're goin' to raise us some of the best horses of Morgan stock in the whole country. We'll have some beef cattle and some milk cows too. I'll raise us a beautiful garden with vegetables and even some flowers, just like Granny Stewart's. Maybe some cockscomb and even some hollyhocks.

We'll have a bunch of beautiful, well-behaved children that we adore. And, Ma, they won't have to run off 'cause we'll treat them right and care about the people they like. You probably won't even see my babies, Ma, 'cause you don't want me. If you don't want me, you won't want my children either. You probably don't even think I can be a good mother." Ruth's tears turned from crying into deep uncontrolled sobbing. The truth was she'd never been so scared or missed her ma more than at this moment.

"You keep telling me I'm just a girl, too little and weak to amount to anything. Well, you're wrong, and I'll prove it. That 'Good Book' you always made me read says I can do all things in Christ who gives me strength if I love Him. Well, I do, so He promised He would help me and never leave me. See, I learned what was taught me, you'll see, Ma."

Emotionally spent, Ruth tried to calm down. She paced back and forth in the dugout shelter they now called home.

The dugout was halfway into the ground. Its windows let a little light in. Mainly, it seemed it let all the dust in. The red dust sifted through the burlap feed sacks Ruth had used as make-do curtains to cover the window openings. A hoe leaned against the corner by the door of the one-room dwellings just in case a snake decided to come in to get out of the heat. It was only May, but the temperatures were already getting very hot during the day. Her worry thoughts returned as she pulled back the burlap and peered out the window to the southwest and noticed the storm bank forming. Ruth knew from growing up in Texas that May and June were the months that storms frequented the Great Plains. With the storms came the twister funnels that sucked up anything they touched. Stories of these big winds claimed even cattle were sometimes picked up out of the prairie and dropped into the next state or territory. Several bad storms from her youth had scared her, even when she was surrounded with loved ones to protect her. Looking out the window, she spoke to her pa as if he was standing beside her, looking at that mean black storm forming.

"Pa, sure am glad you taught me to read the signs. There looks like a storm's a-brewin'."

Storms in the spring came from the southwest and in the winter from the northwest. During the summer, flash floods caused creeks to rise over their banks, filled with debris. Ruth knew the debris was often more dangerous than the floodwaters. It carried poisonous snakes, broken barbed wire, sharp rocks, sewage and mud. Her heart began pounding in her chest and way up into her throat, as she thought about the storm clouds in the distance waiting to dump a deluge of water onto the earth below, causing the yearly flooding.

"Riley, you and Sadie are riding straight in that direction."

Fear of all the what if's and maybe could happens were literally sucking the strength from her body.

"Stop it!" Ruth turned her back to the window.

"I can't be worrin' about everything all the time. After all, it's not pleasing to man nor God to be thinking bad thoughts. I just asked for His protection, now I'll have to have faith and believe my husband and my Sadie will be protected and safe."

Ruth had a habit of thinking out loud whenever no one was around to hear her. She stopped talking and looked around, sensing someone was listening to her rant and rave. A little horned lizard scampered in from the windy out-of-doors. Randomly, Ruth scanned the room to make sure there were no other vermin that might've sneaked in as well. The dwelling that was dug into the ground and covered with sod housed everything from scary spiders, wiggly worms and even snakes.

Back in her parent's house in Texas, her bedroom was larger than this entire dugout. She had had a large bed with a bedspread that matched the curtains. The chamber pot and pitcher with matching basin were made of porcelain and hand painted with Texas yellow roses, like the song. Granny Stewart even had yellow rosebushes planted in the flower beds adorning the large screened-in porch that wrapped around the entire ranch house. Here in the dugout, there was no furniture, only a mat with blankets on the dirt floor and a fire pit at the other end of the room. Noticing the fire pit, she realized she was still holding those two rabbits and began looking for a way to hang them near the door to catch the breeze while avoiding sand blowing all over their carcasses. One of Riley's Bowie knives hung on a peg stuck into the sod wall next to where the gun hung. She took the knife down, hung one rabbit on the peg. The other rabbit she hung off the knife she stuck into the wall. After hanging the rabbits, she felt new energy. Next, she knelt down on the bedding and pulled her big carpet bag over to fetch out her comb and toothbrush. Even though she had no tooth powder, Ruth brushed her teeth vigorously. Next, she combed her hair counting one hundred strokes. With the back of the quilt, she wiped her face and neck and somehow felt cleaner.

Being married to Riley for a short while, she discovered he didn't know what a toothbrush was and hardly knew how to use a bar of soap.

She'd teach him about Dr. Meyers L. Rhein's contraption for cleaning teeth, and Riley could teach her how to love him in all the ways that made him happy.

"Well now, that's more like it. I've said my prayers, cleaned up, now what shall I do?" She looked over where the rabbits were hanging and noticed the flies were starting to gather around the little pool of blood on the dirt floor.

"Oh no, I better clean them, or the flies will make the meat spoil. I think I'll roast one and dry the other as jerky." The wind was still howling, so she did her best to skin those rabbits the way her brother would. The job was done quicker that she thought.

"That was as easy as slipping clothes off a baby." She chuckled at her own little cleverness. Her joy was robbed by the memory of what followed her wanting to learn how to skin wild game. Ruth had asked her pa for a skinning knife so she could learn how to skin and cut up game like her brother did. Pa just shook his head and said,

"Listen little girl, your ma would skin me alive if I let you get all bloody and dirty or lettin' you act like a boy. You scoot on now, you hear me? Let us menfolk do this kind of work, and you keep yourself pretty and clean. But if you really want to help, you can go help set the table and help Granny and your ma."

Her memory faded, and with a toothy grin, she looked at those two rabbits and announced,

"Well Pa, you should see me now. I'm clean and those rabbits are too."

She hurried outside and wiped her hands on the grass like she saw Riley do. She noticed the sky getting darker in the direction Riley and Sadie headed. Her prayers had lost all the formality of church talking prayers and became a running dialogue with her Creator as she would pause to listen to see if He would answer.

"Help me not to worry. Oh, and thank you again for the rabbits." The smile returned to her face.

Before Riley left, he had carried up a large amount of kindling and dried limbs he found down at the creek bed. It was mostly cotton wood that burned quickly. She roasted one rabbit, and the other she cut the meat off the bone into long strips. With her boning knife, she sharpened both ends of several sticks; and in the corner next to the fire pit, she stuck the ends into the wall, creating a drying rack. Carefully, she hung the meat so it wouldn't get any dirt on it. She was thankful that she had remembered to bring a leather pouch of salt and a tin box of black pepper.

She dowsed the jerky liberally with both, which sent her into a sneezing fit. Her eyes now had watery tears from burning caused by the pepper. With difficulty seeing, she did her best to salt the pelts.

"That ought to keep the flies away and help the meat dry."

She was used to doing her work quickly and efficiently. However, today she purposely tried to pace herself to slow down in order to fill her day with meaningful tasks. She wanted her hands and mind busy to keep idleness from leading to worry thoughts.

"Let me think, those furs will come in handy somehow. Maybe I'll make a soft pillow slip for Riley. Even if I don't have enough for two pillows, I can sleep in his arms while he rests on the furry pillow."

This idea brought a smile to her lips. Her emotions had been trotting up and down since Riley and Sadie left. One moment she was down in self pity and the next minute she was thinking of things to do in her husband's absence.

Ruth stepped outside and picked up the water bucket. Taking a sip of water from the gourd dipper, she tasted the muddy grit and spit it out onto the ground. The remaining water was used to wash her hands and knife. Blackness from the horizon was quickly approaching, though the howling winds had steadily calmed down for now. However, the way the clouds looked, she knew the wind could quickly return.

"I better go get some water from the creek before that storm comes to visit. Yes, and I best take that doggone pistol just in case a coyote or something else might be waiting for me at the creek. Hum, let me think, I can't remember. Are coyotes scared of people, or do they eat them? With only two rabbits, I wonder, do people ever eat coyotes?"

Ruth, water bucket in hand, headed to the creek and for the first time this spring, noticed the small prairie flowers and herbs along the way. She gathered several handfuls of sage leaves and put them in the water bucket to keep the water sweet. Purple cone flowers were starting to bloom. She knew they were medicine plants but decided to pick some at another time since it might take both hands to carry her bucket full of water.

The clear creek water was running rapidly. Clear and rapid were good signs that the water was safe to drink. Several willow trees lined the small bank, backed by some taller cottonwood and some other kind of native trees. Twigs, Ruth gleaned from the medicinal willows, she would chew on to relieve her headache caused by the annoying sound of the wind. The more bitter the tree bark of the willow, the stronger the medicine. Granny Stewart had grown up in Scotland and taught Ruth some of the healing arts with herbs and certain minerals. Ruth was happy she had paid attention to her granny. Also, a Comanche woman whom Ruth liked and spoke with often had willingly shared some of her knowledge about animals and plants that lived on the prairie.

Seldom did she go to fetch water; Riley usually did that for her. She heard something plop into the water and surveying where she heard the noise, saw two frog eyes looking up at her from out of the water near the cattail reeds. Suddenly, those frog eyes were violently pulled under as a slither motion broke the surface. It startled her, so she dropped her bucket, turned and ran away. Reason overpowered fear as she remembered her purpose for coming to the creek. As fast as she could run, she returned, snatched the handle of the bucket, filled it, and ran away again. Free from the willow coverage, her attention was drawn to the drama in the sky. Black clouds were churning, mingled with a tinge of gray-green.

"*Oh Pa, that means hail is coming. I better get back to the dugout for shelter.*"

CHAPTER 2

THE STUFF THAT MAKES DREAMS

Ruth's Uncle Wilbur had traveled into Indian territory. He came back with stories, poems and songs about this land where she now lived. He entertained her whole family in the evenings after dinner with his tall tales. On a small piece of paper, he had scribbled Brewster Higley's poem, "The Western Home." This had become her dream of the western home she and Riley would make together.

"Ruthy girl, that land out there is where the deer and the antelope once played as well as the Great American Desert Bison. It's what they call an extirpation. All these animals have either been killed or driven away. I've heard tell that to the northeast, a Scotsman by the name of Duncan has built up a good business trading with the Indians: Comanche, Kiowa, and Apache. The whole area is patrolled by soldiers from the Army Post at Fort Sill. Your pa and me do some horse trading with the Army and with Mr. Duncan. He tells us there is going to be a train coming through those parts one of these days. That land is semi-arid prairie with grass fit only for bison and dirt so full of clay it can't be used for farming, but some of the tribal indigenous people make pots and eating utensils out of it. The sod and clay are used to make houses called dugouts, but it's also a place where rattlers, spiders, scorpions, and centipedes live. Red tailed hawks keep the snake and rabbit population in balance, along with coyotes who eat all kinds of rodents, grasshoppers and snakes. Native herbs, such as purple cone flowers, are used to make powerful medicine to treat venomous bites, sage for treating inflammation and as a culinary herb, arnica to reduce pain and swelling, mullein for coughs and colds, and willow for pain relief. You talk to Arenumi, that Comanche woman our foreman Mack married, and she'll tell

you if you know what you are looking at, just about every plant that grows on the prairie is either food or medicine. Just about everywhere, there are sulfur springs that the Plains people travel great distances to use for their healing waters."

"It's got lots of potential to be a ranching country, but I've also been told that if you stay there long enough, you will learn to love Jesus and hate snakes."

Uncle Wilbur had told that story so many times, Ruth knew it by heart. She remembered everyone would always laugh whenever they heard about lovin' Jesus and hatin' snakes.

Ruth was not laughing now.

Frequently, sitting around the dinner table eating garden- fresh corn, her uncle talked non-stop about his travels. Her pa was unimpressed.

"Now why would anyone in their right mind ever want to live in a God forsaken place like that?" Everyone nodded their heads in agreement with her pa, except she never did. Her uncle made it sound adventurous, a fun challenge; nothing like her life in Texas, where girls couldn't do anything except what they were told to do.

Uncle Wilbur would get in arguments every time he was with his brother.

"John Stewart, you bein' my brother and all, still have to be the most stubborn, narrow-minded, pigheaded man I've ever tried to talk with 'cause you don't use good sense. If it weren't for Ma, your good wife, Molly, and those two youngin's of yours and this delicious food, I might not have the personal restraint to keep from knocking your head off."

This was always the cue for Granny Stewart to come between her boys that towered over her but were powerless in her presence.

"I just keep prayin' that just one meal could be et in this house without someone talkin' about violence. Look at me when I'm talkin' to you. This is no way to behave, and you both know it. You neither will get even a sniff of my bramble cobbler if you don't sit down and finish your dinner like well-bred Scots that you are."

Granny would look over at James and Ruth and wink. That was Ruth's cue to gather up the dinner plates and fetch the cobbler.

Ruth could just about taste the thick, sweet berry filling and the crisp buttery crust of Granny's cobbler as she hurried toward her dugout. Her thoughts made her angry, comparing what she had heard in stories and what she was learning firsthand on her own. Ruth's pa had told her this place was a stormy, windy, scary land in the spring and hot sun-scorched, and prone to prairie fires in the summer; in the autumn, brown with just a touch of orange, gold and a splash of red from the sumac; and cold, windy, and icy in the winter. No wonder men never settled in this place. Maybe her pa was correct, Plains Indians only passed through these lands; outlaws ran away to temporarily hide there. It was only recently the government opened up these lands as free to whoever had enough grit to survive.

"I think ol' Uncle Wilbur sold me a pack of lies."

Riley thought the way her uncle did and had spoken to her with great hope and a plan to farm and ranch this land. He wanted to raise cattle, hogs, chickens, and maybe breed some good Morgan horses. Ruth had told her pa she wanted to raise horses someday. Sadie was given to Ruth as a gift from her pa for just that purpose, but her pa would never have thought she was capable of running off with that Riley hoodlum. What her pa failed to realize was that she shared these dreams of Riley's and they agreed to try their hand at growing cotton and wheat, maybe even alfalfa, peanuts, corn and melons. They were young, in love and determined to make a good life together. So with a heart full of dreams, a wagon loaded with everything they needed, and a carpet bag full of personal belongings, Ruth and Riley crossed the Red River from Texas to claim some free land in Oklahoma as their starting place. It seemed to be full of promise.

* * * * *

Ruth had no idea where Riley was. She was hurrying to get to their dugout for shelter against that big black and greenish cloud moving very quickly in her direction. This sinister storm looked like a dragon in the sky coming right for her. This made her run even faster. About half of the water splashed out of her bucket while hurrying to the dugout. Ruth bent over and stepped through the doorway to see her roasted rabbit moving as ants were consuming it.

"Oh Lord, no! Not my dinner!" She picked the carcass up by one foot and ran outside, shaking it to knock off the ants. Those little biting devils wouldn't shake loose, except for a few that got on her fingers to bite her. Ruth wasn't about to drop the rabbit in the dirt and surrender it so easily. They might bite, but she was bigger than those tiny ants, and she was moved to righteous indignation.

"You can't have my supper!" She yelled at them as if they were interested in what she had to say. She picked up a smooth rock and began smashing them and then caught sight of the bucket of water. She took the whole rabbit, moving with those biting beasts and submerged it in the fresh creek water. Leaving it in the water to drown the army from hell, she dashed inside to get her pouch of salt and box of pepper. Meanwhile, she glanced at the drying jerky that appeared to be free of any vermin. Carefully, she pulled the meat out of the water and proceeded to douse it liberally with salt and then enough pepper to set her off again into a wild sneezing fit.

In a feeding frenzy, Ruth pulled the tough meat off the bones and ate it hungrily. The cool fat liquefied in her hot mouth as she chewed each piece for a long while. The flavor of the rabbit was masked by the drenching of water and seasoning. Taking her greasy hand, she scooped the dead ants out of the water bucket. This left a grease film on the water's surface. The gourd dipper was filled three times to quench her peppery thirst. Ruth drank until her belly felt bloated.

Rain drops the size of silver dollars began to hit her head, but it wasn't until the balls of ice began to bounce off the ground that she sought shelter. The noise was deafening and her breath looked like smoke as the temperature plummeted in a matter of seconds. The clouds blocked out all the sunshine, and in mid-afternoon, it was as dark as night. She picked up her bedding and began shaking the covers just in case there were ants or other crawly things underneath them. Uncomfortably full of meat and water, she sat down in the middle of her covers, alone and chilly with the knowledge that this storm had only just begun.

"I better sleep now, if I can."

She spoke out loud and could hardly hear her own voice over the violence and noise of the hail storm outside.

"God, please keep me safe."

Her thoughts immediately went to her precious Riley and their poor horse. People and animals could be seriously hurt if caught out in a hailstorm. Her pa was always full of such dreadful stories, like the time a man was found on the ground with his head split open. No one was in sight. The hail had already melted and no one could figure out how the man had been murdered. Finally, they surmised he'd been outside in the storm when the fist-sized hailstones fell earlier that day.

"Of all the things Pa taught me, why is it this gruesome story is what I remember right now? Lord, please keep Riley and our horse safe from all

danger. Thank you, I know you will." She eased her head down on the bedding and closed her eyes.

It was the coldness and wetness that woke Ruth. She sat up in the darkness and realized it was night time. Lightning struck nearby and lit the room enough to reveal a puddle of water was invading her blankets. Thunder crashed, followed by more lightning. With the instant illumination from the lightning, she could see outside the wind was blowing the rain horizontally. This violent action was eroding some of the sod bricks, letting in a little stream of water into the dugout. Feeling her way in the dark, she tried to start a fire but discovered all the kindling was wet. Ruth pulled the dry portion of the blanket and wrapped herself with it to stay warm. The crock barrel caught her shin bone and she took advantage of this accident to perch herself on it, keeping her feet off the floor. Looking like some overgrown cocoon, there she slept as best she could until first light. When she opened her eyes, she could hardly move her neck. Her entire body was stiff and achy.

The morning sky was bright and free of clouds before the moon had a chance to leave her night watch. Sunlight peered through one of the holes in the burlap window covering. It was only a pinpoint of illumination in the otherwise dark room, but it hurt Ruth's eyes. Forgetting where she was, she expected to feel Riley's warm body next to hers. Now she remembered; yesterday was not just a bad dream. Still alone, she sighed with regret as she peered out the door. Ruth waded through water to step out of the dugout and found everything drenched by the storm. Some of the hail had not melted but would be gone quickly once the sun heated up the day.

The morning greeted her with a perfect cloudless, magenta-striped azure sky, washed clean and smelling fresh. Ruth always enjoyed the smell of the air after a nasty rainstorm. Frogs had serenaded her to sleep while they were busy laying egg clusters in newly formed puddles the storm prepared. She stood with her blankets still encasing her as she watched the morning sun transform into dawn and scare that lazy moon back to wherever she hid during the day. The pinkish-hue sky gave way to the golden rays cascading from the heavens.

In the brush near the dugout, Ruth heard the quail whistling for bobwhite. Then she noticed butterflies were everywhere. They were what led her eyes to see the plum blossoms covered with butterflies drinking in the sweet nectar. All of nature was happy with the rain- washed air and earth. God in His mercy had sheltered her from the storm and quashed her fears by letting her sleep. This morning, business was as usual for all the critters that shared this land with Ruth. A scissor-tail flycatcher flew close to her showing no fear and began washing in the frog egg pool. Overhead, she heard the cry of another bird. Looking to the sky she squinted to see a red-tailed hawk circling. She felt a peculiar peace at this moment, like singing to the hawk and then to God and even to those little specks of frog eggs that seemed to stare back at her. An inner knowing reassured her all was well. Even when her mind drifted to thoughts of her husband, she seemed to know he was all right, even though she didn't have any idea where he was or if the storm had affected him last night. Ruth wondered how many days it would take before he came home with food. She instinctively looked at the jerky drying. Because of the moisture in the air, the jerky was still sticky to the touch.

After giving thanks for living through the night, Ruth mentally began to plan her day. Her project today was to create some apparatus to move the jerky on to so it could be sheltered from the wind blowing sand yet still take advantage of the warm sunshine. Today, she would fast from food while she searched the area for plants and small game to eat. Her stomach felt sour and bloated from eating all that rabbit and drinking so much water.

The bad news was the condition of everything in the dugout after the storm was soaked from the rain. The good news was the water buckets and small pail were full of fresh water.

"Well, I am happy I won't have to make any trips to the swollen creek today." She pulled off her blankets and laid them on the brush-covered roof of their dugout. She removed all her wet clothes and let them air dry as her body soaked up the warmth of the sunshine and cooled by the morning breeze. She crawled into the flat bed of the wagon and laid down. Out of curiosity, the red-tailed hawk flew close to take a peek at her. Ruth listened to the quail whistling for bobwhite and realized they were very close. Making a mental note to look for their nest, maybe she would find an egg or two and still leave some to hatch. Even a butterfly came to land on her shoulder just to say hello on this fine morning and then quickly returned to the plum blossoms.

"Thank you, my beauty for reminding me that fruit will be available during the summer."

Ruth actually felt refreshed, washed by the water and now sun-dried and warmed. Her damp clothes dried quickly, so she dressed and went inside to tidy up her bedding and repair the wall and water damage

Riley had been gone one day.

CHAPTER 3

EVERYTHING HAS TO EAT

Ruth almost stepped on the little horned lizard that was feeding on the ants she had knocked off the meat yesterday. She liked all kinds of critters and bent down to talk to him.

"I guess you're the closest thing I have to a pet. If you come to live with me, I'll let you eat all the ants out of my house." His eye winked at her. Not knowing anything about the normal antics of lizards, she chose to believe he was in agreement with her proposal.

"Now what shall your name be? If you're to be my pet and confidant, you must have a name. Let's see, you look like…hum…a Samson?" She looked at the lizard, and he turned his head away from her.

"You don't like the name Samson? Well,…hum… what is a good lizard name? Let me think. How about Lawrence the Lizard and we will call you Larry Lizard for short?" Again the lizard turned from her. *"Well, how about Mr. Lizard?"* To this name he ran right up to her and let her pick him up.

"Well now, so Mr. Lizard it is. I find it a little formal, but… if you like it, then Mr. Lizard it'll remain." He scampered off in search of some black ants, which thrilled Ruth. She pulled her carpet bag over to the bed and lined up her hair comb, toothbrush and Bible. Finishing her morning grooming, she opened the Holy Book and began reading it out loud to herself and her new audience.

"Mr. Lizard, the Good Book just says to preach the gospel to all creatures of the world. You're my first creature. Look at you… you are so cute looking up at me whenever I talk to you. You are so ugly you're cute. Let's begin at the beginning, Genesis Chapter 1, In the beginning…"

She read aloud until the time of the Great Flood and then closed the Bible for a time of reflection and prayer.

"Lord, Maker of this great big world, You made everything and called it good. Please show me in this place what's good so I may have something to eat. Will You direct my steps? I want to be brave for Riley and I want to show no fear because that means I really trust You. I do trust You. Please help me whenever I forget to trust You... please? I promise to fast today since I ate that whole rabbit and feel so bloated, but tomorrow will You show me what to eat? Please watch over Riley and our Sadie. Thank You for Mr. Lizard. I can now talk to You and Your little spiny creature whom You sent to keep the ants and other vermin off my food that You are going to provide for me. Lord, I mean no disrespect but may I ask a question for some clarification? Before I read about the Great Flood and the story of Noah bringing all the animals two by two, You promised with Your rainbow in the sky that You would never destroy the world by using flooding. So if Mr. Lizard doesn't understand, may I have Your permission to explain that this last flood is not the end of the world but just a major inconvenience? Amen."

All day long she busied herself with repairing the dugout and making a plan of things that needed to be done. She tried her best to drink plenty of water and to keep her mind off food. About mid-afternoon, she ran out of energy and decided to take a nap for a couple of hours. When Ruth awoke, she read until sunset. She tried to sleep again but did so fretfully. Ruth was awake long before daylight, so she remained in her warm covers until the sun was completely up. A fire was lit, and then some water was put on to boil the leftover bones of the rabbit. She stepped outside and gathered some more sage and grass roots to help make a broth. With a little salt and pepper, she was surprised how good it tasted. If the rabbit had only been mutton and a slip of carrot, turnip, cabbage, and shelled peas were added with maybe a spoonful of dried barley, it would taste just like Granny Stewart's Scotch Broth. This had been a family recipe for as far back as 1786, at least that was when it had actually been written down and placed into a book. Each day she made a little soup using some of the rabbit jerky. Because seasonings were limited, she tried to be creative and used plum blossoms one day, sage the next, some wild garlic and other sweet grasses to add some variety and flavor to the bland soup.

Granny Stewart was the best cook. She always was baking berry tarts or griddle scones. She loved to make Scottish Shortbread to have with her tea. Around the holidays, there was always Oatmeal Gingerbread made with that combination of molasses and syrup known as black treacle and

17

ginger. Honey and Whiskey Cake was her pa's favorite anytime of the year. Her older brother, James, would pick brambleberries and peaches just so he would have Granny Stewart make cobblers with them. Her ma said the best pie in the world was Granny's Buttermilk Pie. Granny Stewart made jams and jellies, and she canned pickles from melon rinds as well as cucumbers. Nothing better than swinging in the tall tree while munching on one of Granny's bread and butter pickles.

Also, Granny could make just about anything using oats. Granny would make black and white pudding, an old dish common in Scotland. It was more like a type of sausage than pudding. The white was made with meat and oatmeal but the black was made with blood and oatmeal. It was an acquired taste that only Pa and Granny would share. Ma claimed she was made to eat it as a child, and since she was a grown person, she didn't have to eat it anymore.

Ruth loved Apple Spice Cake and hot oatcakes off the griddle with fresh cottage cheese and treacle drizzled over them. She could eat three oatcakes at one meal.

In the kitchen, Granny would sing using words nobody understood, but the songs were pretty. When Ruth asked her granny what those words were, Granny would wipe her eyes with the edge of her apron and tell her beloved granddaughter it was an ancient language that was best sung rather than spoken. She said she was born in a far off land called Caledonia, but now, she was proud to be in America, where everyone had food to eat and more than one dress to wear. She was happy to eat cornbread or spoon bread, as she called it, so she didn't have to make everything out of oats. She loved potatoes, so she didn't have to eat just turnips like she did in the old country.

Ruth didn't know how old her granny was and she didn't care. Young in heart and light on her feet she was, and Granny Stewart didn't care who knew it. Ruth started dancing around the dugout just like her Scottish granny used to do to the fiddle music at the socials. Her granny didn't care she didn't have anyone to dance with; she said they would only slow her down.

"I wonder if where I am right now is in America? If it is, then there has to be food, 'cause Granny said so. Boy, do I miss you Granny. Thinking about all your good cookin' makes my mouth water and my stomach growl. I got to think about something else right now."

The weather was warm enough to start a garden with the seeds they brought from Texas. Yesterday's fasting was behind her. Almost shaky with hunger, she remembered what her pa had emphatically taught her about never eating the planting seed. He'd say:

"I don't care how hungry you think you are. Do not eat your planting seed. If you do, it'll only feed you for one meal, whereas if you plant it and make a good crop you'll be fed for the next year."

Ruth pulled out the bags of seed and opened each to see how they looked. One corn kernel and a few peas were withdrawn and without guilt, she quickly threw them into her rabbit broth, just for some variety. Outside, the soil was moist enough for her to cultivate it with the hoe.

"Now how does that planting song go? Let me think. Granny used to sing it to me. Hum, can't even remember the tune but it had something to do with sowing peas and beans during the waning of the moon. 'Who soweth them sooner soweth too soon,' that's it!"

The next three days were spent making a beautiful vegetable garden. She planted mostly corn, okra, turnips, mustard greens, beets, tomatoes, peppers, carrots, parsnips and squash. She knew that this sign of the moon would help the young plants prosper. She decided to plant the three types of beans and peas after the full moon as Granny's song suggested.

On the fourth day she collected rocks and created a neat border around the garden. She spoke to every seed and thanked them for being unique and wonderfully made by the same Creator who created her. She told each one they were delicious, and she looked forward to having them for dinner.

"God, thank You! I know it was Your perfect plan for us to walk with You in a garden. Let's You and me walk in this garden and become really good friends. I appreciate the fact I have everything to learn. You have taught the plants and animals how to live and what to eat so I am confident that You know everything and will teach me what I need to know. I'm just so happy with my first garden and Riley will be so pleased."

On the fifth day, it rained. It rained most of the seed to the surface and rolled most of the rocks away. She was awakened by the cawing sound of three crows eating the corn seed. She dashed out of the doorway with arms waving to frighten the crows but slipped in the mud and sat down hard. The crows never even moved and continued to eat. They reluctantly flew away when she began to throw handfuls of mud at each of them.

"Lord, first the ants and now the crows…Am I being punished? Oh God, it is no use. This is just too hard. I'm sick to my stomach. I'm so hungry. I

might as well have eaten that corn rather than feed the birds with it. This just makes me mad. I'm angry God! Where is Riley? Dang him, anyway!"

She tried to get up but slipped again, falling this time on her face. Mud was everywhere: in her hair, on her clothes, on her face, in her ears, up her nose.

"If you're doing this to humble me, it's working. I feel so defeated. Riley's been gone almost a week now. Lord, is Riley dead? Has he just left me out here to die of starvation? Is this some horrible trick to get rid of me? You know, come to think of it, he was sure in a hurry to leave me, and he said he was going hunting. Well, I bet he's in some nice house, sleeping in a real bed, eating fried chicken right now. Whatever he's doing, he's not here doing it with me!"

She finally made it to her feet and struggled to get out of the mud and onto the grass. The grass was still wet with rain water, and she used it to wipe her hands and face to remove the mud as best she could.

"That darn fool ought to be glad he's not with me right now 'cause if he was I'd...I'd...beat him up. I'd find a stick and hit him with it. Why, I'd throw mud in his face. I'd take his belt and hide it so his pants would fall down. That...would...look...kind...of... funny, now, wouldn't it? Yes sir, I'd hide his boots too!"

She started laughing and couldn't quit. She rolled in the tall grass laughing at the sight she saw in her mind. Those pictures faded and were replaced with pictures of her darling husband hurt and helpless. Those laughs quickly turned to sobs. The weeping sapped her energy. Rolling onto her back, she looked up at the sky.

"Lord, You're showing me the truth of what's happened, aren't You? I got to be the meanest, most horrible person in the world. I deserve this hellhole. I can't do anything right. That's why Ma and Pa were always fussing at me. They don't hate me. They're just disappointed in me. Riley came along, and he liked what he saw...at least he said he did. He trusted that I'd be strong and get by while he was gone. Now he's probably hurt bad, and all that's hurt on me is my feelings. Forgive me, Lord. I don't want to be thinking ugly thoughts about Riley, my folks, or even those stupid crows that are just out here surviving like I'm trying to do."

Ruth stopped talking out loud and retreated to the privacy of her own thoughts but the ugly thoughts just wouldn't go away.

She had always been small for her age. Pa was a mountain of a stout and sturdy Scotsman. He and his kin were all rock-solid muscle men who lived larger than life. Life was meant to be conquered more than enjoyed. A challenge once met was instantly replaced with a more difficult challenge, so no one would ever question their breed was the best of the best. James was just like his ma and pa. He knew most of the Bible by heart before he turned twelve years old. He was an accomplished horseman and seemed to be able to charm the milk cows to give more milk. Each morning, he woke up before anyone in the house just to light the stove so Granny or Ma would have it hot to cook breakfast for the family.

Her ma was thin and bouncing with excess energy. Ma's sister Aunt Clara shook her head in amazement as she told Ruth about the day her ma gave birth to her.

"I never saw anything like it. Why, did you know your ma hung out an entire line of wet clothes to dry in the sunny breeze then went inside to suckle you. Lord, I sure never could've done that."

Whether it was cooking or housework, sewing or music, her ma would brag to others how well Ruth did, but that was just a lie. Time and again she found her cookies thrown to the chickens and another batch made to replace them while Ruth slept. She could tell the difference in the morning that the cookies were definitely her ma's because she just did everything better.

She found her ma insincere whenever she was appearing to boast about her actions to neighbors or friends at church. Ruth felt as if her ma had to make her more like she wanted a perfect daughter to be. Instead of pride, Ruth only heard sad disappointment in the tone of her ma's voice.

However, Ruth wasn't sure what to think of her pa's opinion. No matter what she said about anything, he was there to correct her. Ruth was thinking of the time she commented to her pa how beautiful the full moon was, and he didn't even look but retorted that he had seen better when he visited up in Missouri. That pretty much summed up every conversation she tried to have with her pa.

As she grew older it became just too tiresome to try to have a conversation with him or to try to please her ma. Even the young people at church looked past her whenever she came to the meetings. Oh, they were polite enough. She just didn't feel like she belonged somehow. Ruth never excelled at anything she had ever done. Nobody cared what she thought. She knew that for sure. Her brother, James, reinforced that to her enough times.

"Ruthy, nobody gives a diddle-darn what you think. Just keep your mouth shut and look pretty. Is that so hard to do?"

Aroused again by emotion, she spoke loudly to her emotionally and physically distant relatives.

"Yep, my family is just too wonderful for words. Then, James, your baby sister had to come along and couldn't do a blamed thing right. You claimed I was dropped on my head one too many times. You called me stupid because I tripped over my skirt coming out of the chicken coop and dropped all the eggs. You told everyone at church about that and claimed someone left a baby on the doorstep 'cause no Stewart could be so clumsy. Everyone had a big laugh and Pa and Ma wouldn't even look at me. Granny would come to my room and I'd cry and she would pet my hair and sing something to me in words I didn't understand. She'd bring me some sweet milk and a little bite to eat whenever I was sent to my room without supper for doing something stupid. I'm nothing but a big disappointment to you all, except for Granny. But then she died and I was really alone."

Ruth felt her insides were balling up into a knot and couldn't tell if she was starting her monthly cycle or just starving. She flopped down into her covers, closed her eyes and fell into a twilight type sleep and began to dream.

Her granny was sitting at the edge of her bed, and it was in her parent's house where she grew up in Texas. Everything was clean, the window was open and a breeze was making her curtains flutter. Granny's hands were cool on her hot forehead. She was humming an old Scottish tune that didn't have any lyrics.

"Granny, am I going to die?"

"Oh my sweet wee one, you are going to die someday but not today. You have just passed from childhood into womanhood. The hurt won't last, nor the bleedin'. You can be happy and sad today. You are no longer a child, but God's makin' you ready for a wee baby to come grow inside ya someday. Here now, drink some of my herb tea and the crampin' will lessen. You will sleep and wake up feeling better. We will talk more about this later."

"But Granny, I'm just a girl, how can I be a woman now? I don't like this. Ow, my tummy hurts."

"Shh now, drink your tea. You're a strong one; you'll get through this and be stronger for it."

"But Granny..."

"Take a sip, I put some honey in it, just for you."

Ruth opened her eyes and remembered the scene like it was yesterday.

"I could barely hear what she was whispering, then it donned on me, she was praying for me. I wish my dear Granny was praying for me now."

Ruth really missed her Granny. She was a hard worker with a do-it-once-and-do-it-right philosophy."

Ruth thought for a long while about her dreams and all the things she had seen others accomplish and decided the philosophy of "do it once and do it right" might have some exceptions to it, like planting her garden. She heard her stomach growling and couldn't ignore it.

"What I would give for a fresh peach right off the tree." Her lizard friend stopped to listen. She picked up the horned creature and gently stroked his belly.

"You know what else I'd give anything for right now? A big feather pillow, the kind Granny made me with goose down." The lizard had closed his eyes, totally relaxed. That pillow of hers was propped up on her bed at home. How many times had she cried herself to sleep using that pillow as a big sponge? She wondered if her ma had cried from missing her. She wasn't sure.

"Well, there is no sponge in this place. That's the truth," she said still talking to the sleeping pet. She laid him on the ground, and he came to life, scampering off to find more ants. She promised that today she would not cry and made a mental commitment to sing some happy songs to help pass the time.

"For the life of me, I can't... I can't think of one happy song. All the songs that come to mind are about Jesus dying or about losing your true love. Hum, let me think now. I can sing Jimmy Crack Corn but I Don't Care.

She began to sing:

"When I was young I used to wait on Master and hand his plate
Pass him the bottle when he got dry and brush away the blue-tail fly.
Jimmy crack corn and I don't care. Jimmy crack corn and I don't care...
No, that's a stupid song. If that ol' song writer don't care; why should I?"

The self-talk was not working to improve her mood. Her gloomy moods were usually resolved by sleep. In the heat of the afternoon, she would become drowsy. If she slept the afternoon away, she would be awake in the middle of the darkness. Even though the light was not particularly her friend, the dark was definitely her enemy.

"What would I be doing right now if I were home?"

It took her a while to think.

"I'd be sewing."

That thought gave her an idea. Ruth looked for her satchel, which held her needle and thread. Finding both, she tore a large portion of cloth from her petticoat. Sewing two of the sides together, she made a pouch: the beginning of a pillow.

"What will I fill this with to make it a soft pillow for sleep?"

Her thoughts returned to the Texas house of her youth and to her ma.

"Ma, I wish I could have pleased you with my sewing. This will be my finest work and I will embroidery 'Riley loves Ruth' on the front. It will be big enough both our heads will fit on it. Hum, if not, I will sleep in his arms and he can use it under his head."

Carefully Ruth made small even embroidery stitches to form the letters R I L E Y. Cutting the thread with her teeth, she put the needle away and carried her pillow outside in search of stuffing material. The brightness made her shield her eyes. Everything was engulfed in light.

The prairie was alive with new growth from the spring rains. Seeing the sweet grass, she began gathering handfuls to fill her pillow. All she had to do was sew up the end, and Riley would have a gift made just for him when he arrived home.

Ruth sat down, and several quail flew out of their hiding place. They probably scared her more than she scared them. However, soon she was calm again, soaking in the warmth of the sunshine and intrigued with the different earthy smells that made her feel like she was part of this place: the land, sky, animals and plants. For the first time since Riley had gone hunting, she didn't feel lonely.

* * * * *

It was the buzzing in her ear from a honey bee that woke her, and she sat up with a start. Ruth had no memory of falling asleep in the tall grass. Her pillow was beautiful and filled with sweet smelling grass. She admired the stitching of her embroidery and ran her finger lightly over it just to feel the texture. The sun had come out and dried up the grass, her clothing and most of the puddles in her garden. She got to her feet and found a stick and walked over to the garden and started poking seeds deeper into the ground. Tomorrow she would find more stones and repair the border. As she walked away from the dugout to relieve herself, she almost stepped on a little nest of quail eggs. No mama quail was sitting on them, so she reached down and picked out two of the four that were in the nest. She wanted all four, but that would not be fair. Hurrying back to the house, she started a fire and cooked the eggs. Mr. Lizard was feasting on ants while she ate. Those quail eggs were possibly the most delicious eggs she had ever tasted.

"Did you know, Mr. Lizard, in some places in this world quail eggs are quite the delicacy? Yes, they are. Some are pickled. My ma said she saw some in a jar one time in Kansas City at a fancy lady's house where she used to work. They even ate black fish eggs. It has a fancy name, but I can't remember what it is. Hum…some people eat snake. I guess if you were hungry enough you could eat anything. Mr. Lizard, I think I could eat snake. Oh don't look at me that way; I'd never eat you…maybe." She started laughing again at her funny little thoughts.

CHAPTER 4

PREPARE FOR BATTLE

Riley had been gone for over three weeks now, when she had the opportunity to taste cooked snake. Ruth was out in the garden admiring the little corn shots and the peas and beans that had broken the surface and were holding their own against two additional thunder storms. She was leaning up against her hoe when she heard the rattle. There it was not a foot away: coiled tight, sticking its forked tongue out at her, and rattling its tail. They made eye contact, then it sprung at her with its mouth open and fangs extended. Instinctively, she pivoted away as one of its fangs caught the hem of her skirt. Her movements were as calm and controlled as if she had been trained in the ancient Oriental Art of Warfare. The curve of the hoe that attached to the handle lifted the snake's body off her skirt while Ruth used the hoe as a bat to send that poor rattler into the air. When it landed on the ground and was slithering away from her, she chased it down and chopped it in half. In one movement she chopped the head off and flicked it into the tall grass. When she looked down at her skirt, the hem was spattered with white milky venom. Picking up the snake she had severed with the hoe, she began talking to it like the defeated foe it had become.

"You *might have had big fangs with poison that could kill me with one bite, but I have a mouthful of teeth that are now going to eat you. I am going to keep your rattler as my personal trophy. Jesus told us in the scriptures that those people who loved Him would be able to handle snakes and drink poison. If I don't get some fresh water today, that stuff in the water bucket may just turn into poison."*

She roasted the snake and ate it for supper. Ruth remembered a discussion she and her family had had around the dinner table when she was young. Her brother James began:

"Why, there's nothing wrong with eating snake meat, an old lady at church told me it tastes just like chicken."

Ruth thought on that as she was chewing the rubbery meat. She pretended to be speaking to this lady- whoever she was- from church who knew all about snake meat.

"Madam, you said this tastes just like chicken. I suggest you check your chickens because something terrible has happened to your sweet chickens to make them taste like snake!"

She started laughing and then got the hiccups. After she calmed down, the decision was made to throw the snake bones away and not use them for broth. The thought of broth slithering down her throat made her feel uneasy.

* * * * *

With some protein in her belly, sleep came easy for her. In the morning, she rolled over and made a mark on the floor and then counted them. Riley had been gone twenty-five days. The weather had been unseasonably stormy this spring, and she knew, using good reason, he was unable to return to her because of the swollen creeks and rivers. Their creek was maybe four times its normal width, and it had already begun to meander into some smaller tributaries. Snakes, frogs and birds seemed to be more visible- all signs of heavy rain. Her garden was growing remarkably well because of the moisture in the evenings and the bright sunshine in the mornings. The fact of waking up wet was beyond annoying, so she took to sitting up during the stormy nights, listening to the maddening wind, then climbing up into the wagon in the morning and sleeping in the warmth of the sunshine. She still tried to groom herself, but it just wasn't worth stepping into the murky swollen waters of the creek to bathe or spend the energy to haul water to wash her hair.

A dear friend had once told her how to clean her hair in a surprising way. Her friend was named Arenumi, which means red smoke. Arenumi, who grew up following the buffalo on the Great Plains, married Sebastian McCormack. She met Mack, as he was called, when he was a soldier at Ft. Sill. She and some other Comanche survivors of an attack on their tribe traveled behind the cavalry to relocate and become educated by

27

missionaries. She learned to speak perfect English and to dress and behave as a white woman. Nevertheless, the U.S. Army discharged Mack for marrying an Indian. They left Ft. Sill and traveled with John Stewart back to his ranch in Texas, after he sold the Army some fresh horses from his herd. Mack was hired on as foreman for Ruth's family on their ranch in Texas. This is how Ruth came to meet the foreman's wife. Ruth became friends with Arenumi, who taught her many helpful things to know about living on the prairie from the Numinu or Comanche tribe. Today Ruth used Arenumi's instruction on how to clean her hair without using water. Arenumi had beautiful glossy black hair *(paapi* as she called it). It was always neatly braided and never looked dirty. But dirt was what she used to keep it clean. Once a week, she would dust her hair with finely powdered dirt. Then she would sit and comb her long locks until all the excess oil was removed and with it the dirt. When Ruth followed her instruction, it worked just like Arenumi said it would. But Ruth had been losing quite a bit of hair every morning. She had begun to notice a fine downy growth of hair on her face and body even though the hair on her head was thinning. Her tongue was sore, and her eyes were producing more and more discharge. The cracks in the corners of her mouth stung when the sweat from her head trickled down her cheeks or whenever the salt in her tears fell on her lips. She also noticed her toothbrush was bloody after each brushing and the inside of her mouth was covered with sores. Already slender, her current weight loss was revealing her rib bones and knobby knees. As her body continued to break down due to lack of nourishment, she gleaned more information from the recesses of her memory that was deposited by stories shared by Granny Stewart and Arenumi.

Ruth sat combing her hair remembering how she loved visiting Arenumi. Often, they would ride their horses together, and Arenumi would tell her stories she learned from her grandmother, and Ruth would share some of Granny Stewart's tall tales.

Ruth believed her friend was the happiest person she knew. Arenumi was at ease with everything around her. She was at ease with herself. This amazing woman talked to everything just like it understood her. Only sometimes she talked to certain animals and birds speaking in Numic, her first language, that of the Comanche. When asked why she didn't speak English to the animals, Arenumi told Ruth that hummingbirds didn't understand English but red tailed hawks understood every language, animal and human. Insects, Arenumi believed, would not listen to any man's language because they owned this earth and found man to be alien. That was why, according to Arenumi, insects were always at war with the human race.

Calla was the name of Arenumi and Mack's dog. She understood everything humans said to her in English and Numic. Calla was the first animal Ruth understood by her noises and antics. Her belly was full of puppies when Ruth first met Calla. She promised Ruth she could take care of one of her daughters when all her puppies were old enough to leave her. Even though Ruth's ma wouldn't let her have a puppy, Ruth begged every day for a week. Her ma said Buster, the ranch cow dog was all they needed.

"No Ruthy, I said no and that is final. Those mutt-type Indian dogs cannot be trained. They just go around killing whatever they see to eat. I'm afraid one of those puppies- I don't care how smart she is- will get into the hen house and steal some eggs or kill the chickens. Why, Eleanor Murphy was telling me they are part fox. Anyway, you know foxes love to eat chickens."

Since Ruth couldn't have a puppy, she would ride her horse, Sadie, to the edge of the property where Arenumi and Mack lived. She would go in and eat some food with them and stay a while and play with the puppies. Mack was kin to Granny Stewart somehow. Knowing Granny the way Ruth did, this might be so or it might not. She had a habit of collecting people along the way and treating them all like family. Ruth liked that about Granny. The truth be known, she liked everything about Granny.

"Granny, I miss you every day of my life. I wish you were here with me right now."

At that moment, Ruth smelled a hint of rosewater in the air. That was Granny Stewart's perfume and she always smelled good, like rose petals.

Rose petals! That reminded Ruth of another piece of wisdom Arenumi taught her.

Ruth remembered one morning when Arenumi was up at their ranch house trimming the rosebushes, she began gathering the rose hips. Holding her hand out to Ruth, Arenumi shared handfuls of the bulbous part of the withered rose bloom. They tasted good, somewhat sweet and tart.

"You eat, Ruth, they make skin and mouth feel good and keep from getting sores."

Ruth thought she had seen some wild roses near the creek that were giving way to the hot weather and were starting to form their own rose hips. Carrying her carpet bag, Ruth walked to where she thought they were; and much to her delight, there were many rose hips, bright reddish orange, hanging like berries on the rose bush branches. Ruth gathered some but remembered Arenumi's instruction to leave plenty for later. She grazed on the pulpy portion and spit out the seeds on the ground at the base of the roses. It was amazing. Her mouth and gums instantly began to feel better.

"I thank God for these rose hips and their medicine."

A honey bee buzzed past her face and drew attention to a swarm dancing among the roses and working their way back and forth to the bee hive. This ancient bee drama intrigued her, and while watching, she noticed other trees next to the willows by the creek. Now that she was closer to them, she noticed for the first time there was some sort of fruit or nut clinging to the branches. Ruth was pleased she remembered to bring her carpet bag to gather herbs and whatever she found edible. Much to her surprise, the ground at the base of the largest tree was covered with what appeared to be native pecans. Two squirrels were watching her and became alarmed at her discovery, which they thought was their secret. They started making all sorts of racket when she approached them.

"Don't be making such a fuss. I'm not going to rob you of all your winter treasure. I'm going to gather up enough to enjoy. I'm really robbing these nut from the worms."

Indignant, the squirrels shook their tails at her and ran up the tree out of sight. There were more than enough for the squirrels and their family and for Ruth's needs. She grew tired of picking and stopped when her large bag was half full. The pecans left her hands and fingernails completely black. She tried to crack one of the nuts with her teeth but feared her tooth would crack before the nut would. Instead, she took them back to the wagon and cracked two handfuls using the butt of her heavy knife. She roasted them in the sun and ate them that evening. These welcomed treats of nuts and rose hips made her very thirsty and she needed to make another trip to the stream for some fresh water.

A red tailed hawk was flying overhead, spying on Ruth gathering the rose hips and pecans. She must have had a nest nearby because she seemed to always be hunting overhead. On the way to the creek for water, Ruth walked up on the hawk with a newly killed pheasant. When the hawk saw Ruth, she took to flight leaving the pheasant for Ruth's supper.

"Oh my, thank you God for sending this hawk to be my hunter friend." Looking up into the sky she waved at the hawk as the thermals carried the bird effortlessly higher above the clouds.

"*Thank you! My name for you my hunter friend will be Helper. I am so happy right now I am going to do a happy dance to honor you, my new friend.*"

As Ruth danced she began to sing a spontaneous song to the red-tailed hawk.

"Oh my sister, my friend, my Helper,
Lift your wings and catch the breeze.
Go fly through the sky
Go look beyond and spy
And find my love, and find my love.
Tell him I am waiting
But not so paitently and return him to my arms
And the fire in my heart.
Is it too much to ask, Lord,
To make me a red-tailed hawk
With wings so strong that I may fly, fly beyond
My prayer is for Mr. Sun to return his light
So my life may go on and on,
That my love can find his way
And be lost from me no more.
So my love, oh, (sigh)
So he can be lost no more."

Ruth spread her arms out like wings and ran, jumping into the air as if she could take off and fly. She then reached down and picked up the pheasant and held it up to show God her gratitude. Back to the dugout she went to build a fire and to roast her fine dinner. She felt a reverence and new respect for this gift of food. Not one bit of it would be wasted. The feathers would be used as a fan to help cool her during the heat of the day and she planned to sew some to her dress to cover up some holes and tears in the fabric.

Looking down at the large female pheasant, she remembered her uncle bringing her ma a burlap game bag full of pheasants. Ma roasted them with current jelly until the skin was crispy sweet. Her ma seemed to think the females were the best eating birds, but the males had the prettier feathers. As she inspected the fowl, it had a healthy amount of fat on it. Her ma had always remarked how rich- meaning fatty- the females could be and would save some of its fat for other meals. Ruth spoke aloud to herself:

"Don't eat too much of this rich meat at one seating or it might make me sick."

It had been a long while since she had eaten any fat, and although she craved it, Ruth was determined to use good sense and stay well. As it were, her body fat was dwindling. Even in the heat of the day, her hands and feet were always cold. Arenumi came to mind again. She made sure Mack and the ranch hands always carried a canteen of water and some pemmican with them whenever they were out in the prairie rounding up steers. Pemmican was a meat jerky-type food that didn't spoil and would keep the men from getting hungry until they could come back to the ranch for a meal. Ruth wished she had brought some with her to keep her from being so hungry. Her body was craving fat and protein, so she decided to dry some of the pheasant and save the meat to make pemmican. This would stretch out the protein and fat for her. She would limit herself to eat small portions daily until it was all gone.

* * * * *

Just about every other day, Ruth would make a new promise to God, if only He would bring her husband back home to her. She would stop her complaining and go through the list of blessings and this would give her cheer until her energy ran out.

"Well, think of it this way. Nobody at home would ever think that skinny Ruth would ever live for twenty- five days with so little to eat. Now I am feasting on pheasant, quail eggs, roasted rabbit, rose hips, pecans, soup and an assortment of wild herbs. I have my own personal pet to keep my dwelling free from pests and vermin, what more could I ask for? Oh, I better not ask that question, I'll lose my happy mood." She stopped talking out loud and retreated to the silence of her own thoughts.

As much as she continued to promise to stop thinking ugly thoughts, they seemed to just pop into her mind without any invitation. At times she wasn't quite sure if she was asleep dreaming or just having conversation in her imagination. Some of her thoughts were memories, and some were made up by the anger that was festering within her heart. Anger was beginning to calcify into bitterness. Ruth heard Granny Stewart's voice. Yes, she remembered that day, this was a memory. Yes, this really happened. Yes, she willed herself to relive the moment within her memory.

"Oh my wee lass, Ruthy-girl, stop your cryin', Love."

"Granny, my heart hurts, my stomach refuses food and my eyes just can't quit cryin'."

"Can you find words to tell me what's grievin' you so?"

"I wish I'd never been born. That's what's grievin' me so. James can do not one blessed thing wrong in Ma's and Pa's eyes, and I can't even eat my porridge properly. I had the bad manners of stirring my oatmeal rather than spooning them through the cool cream. After breakfast, Ma was plaiting my hair, and she yanked it so hard I have a sore where she ripped it out by the roots. Yes, it hurts and yes, I wanted to cry, but I didn't. Ma would have just scolded me to stop cryin,' or she would give me something to cry about. Granny, last night she saw me talking to a boy, a friend of James. He asked me if I knew where James was, and I answered I didn't know. Well, she took hold of my ear and told me she was going to beat the lust out my eyes. Pa made her stop when she took the stick to me. I still had to soak my petticoats in cold water to get the bloodstains out of them. Oh Granny, I know she is not your daughter, but you could talk to Pa? He would listen to you. Granny, when I'm old enough, I'm goin' to run off and never come back. That should finally make Ma happy.

"Oh child, those are hateful thoughts and words. She is wrong to hurt you and you are wrong to hate her. At my age, darling Ruth, I've been on both sides of it, the hatin' and the hurtin'. I can't rightly make no reason of it, child, 'cause these are unreasonable deeds."

"Granny, why does she hate me?"

"Oh, darlin' girl, hate is just the disguise. It's fear and anger she's puttin' onto you. You were so little, just a wee tiny baby. Everyone at church told her she was havin' another boy. Oh, my Johnny was such a large baby, he almost killed me birthin' him. But you were neither big or a boy. She was scared you might not live and then she was scared you might live and not be right in the head. And when you were strong and healthy, then a new fear took those two fears away. You did live, and you turned out to be more beautiful than your ma. Your pa favored you, and all the rest of the kin kept speaking that ol' foolish Scottish curse over ya."

"Curse? What are you talkin' about? What on Earth are you talkin' about, Granny?"

"Oh, that a beautiful daughter is a curse to her mother. She'll draw men to her for her beauty and never amount to anything other than the charms she can give to lustful men. She can never be a proper wife and never care for her elder kinfolks."

Ruth hung her head, feeling deeply defeated. Ruth believed she was a huge disappointment to her mother and Ruth had no clue how to change her predicament.

"Granny, what can I do? Am I cursed?"

"Oh, heavens, no! Listen to me child. No one should ever pretend to think that children are theirs to make them perform the way they want them to perform. Oh, the best any parent can hope for is to teach them manners, obedience and the fear of God. I'm a firm believer that kindness and love is the best way to rear younguns. Teach them to love God with all their heart, mind, soul and strength and then they don't have to beat the devil out of 'um every day. Ruth, our Lord commands us to love Him and one another. Personally, I don't have a bit of trouble lovin' the Lord, but I do have trouble lovin' some of His children. That's why I ask for His forgiveness every day. It's a hard command, Ruthy-girl, but He tells us if we don't love others, even those who hurt us, we really don't have any part of Him in us. Child, my sweet adorable girl, you can hate the wrong your parents do, but don't hate them. Our Lord is not done workin' on you or your folks neither. You best chew on those words for a while 'cause He done told me this so I could tell you. I reckon I needed to be reminded myself, that's why He used me to tell you."

Ruth listened but she was not amused by her Granny's counsel then nor was she any happier to hear it again in her memories. Oh she recognized the truth when she heard it, she just wasn't ready to stop feeling angry and self-righteous. One thing she did share with her ma was stubborn pride. She wore that pride like an elegant gown covering her entire being. Ruth was not finished picking her wounds and her self-pity kept those wounds from healing. In a loud proud voice she spoke to the wind as if it would carry her message to all her wrong-doers in her past.

"If you could see me now, you wouldn't treat me like I don't exist! All you people that treat me like I am some sort of house pet that you just feed and water and pat on the head. Well, I'm not! I'm a real live snake fighting, house building, storm surviving prairie woman who can do anything God gives me the strength to do."

So proud of herself and her bold speech, she began prancing around. Ruth stopped and curtsied to an invisible audience. Looking up into the vast blue sky, Ruth suddenly felt shallow and arrogant. Her spirit knew the truth: the food today, every day was given to her. There was no hunting or farming for what she received. Her mind realized what her spirit knew, everything was a gift. No longer did she feel small in this great universe. Instead, Ruth felt amazed, cared for, really loved and above all grateful. Now she understood that she was not surviving on her own. She was not alone.

Ruth felt grateful for the sunshine of summer, even if it was taking over the coolness of spring time. With hot weather came a new set of challenges: bugs, gnats, flies, fleas, chiggers, mosquitoes. Every bug that liked to bite was taking up residency in and around the dugout. With her new attitude of gratitude, she was being tested on how she would be grateful for this next life challenge that came with living on the prairie.

What Ruth was not quite prepared for was the swarm of grasshoppers. They came in on the wind one hot afternoon. She was struck with horror as she looked at her beautiful vegetable garden that was just about to start producing edible food. The corn had not tasseled but the peas and beans were almost big enough to eat.

When Ruth saw the swarm cloud of grasshoppers coming in her direction without thought, she dropped to her knees and began to pray and weep to the Lord. Before her eyes, an army of crow and various other birds seemed to come out of nowhere. The battle began as Ruth ran to the dugout and gathered up all her blankets and clothes and threw them over her tender plants. The grasshoppers started dropping out of the sky and onto her head, down her blouse and hopping up her shirt. This sent her into a frenzy, smashing them with her feet and chopping them with her hoe. The birds circled and dove out of the sky as winged-eating monsters. The wind shifted in direction, and what seemed to be a war of doom suddenly changed with the wind. Ruth stood in a state of shock, surrounded by dead grasshopper bodies. Mr. Lizard was crunching on grasshopper body parts. He actually looked like he was smiling.

"Look at you, my little friend, you won't be hungry for the rest of the summer. Shall I look under the covers and see what the damage is?" Very slowly she pulled back the covers and smashed a few insects that had made it into her garden. It was amazing. The crops had been spared. This was an undeniable miracle. Grasshoppers just ate everything and didn't leave until all vegetation was consumed. Not today. The mysterious wind and the large flock of birds had come and saved her food source.

She ran into the dugout, pulled her Bible out from under the mat and returned with it to the garden. With the Holy Book open to Joshua 1:9, she walked the border of the garden, reading out loud. Then turning to Joel 2 that described the army of Locusts and God's deliverance, she yelled the words of victory up to the heavens. Marching around and around the rocked border of the garden she read Psalms and sang praises to her beloved Lord who spared the crops. She was singing one minute and weeping in gratitude the next. This act of mercy touched her deeply and out of her spirit sprung renewed faith and trust in a loving God, her God in time of trouble. This was a God who really cared for her. To some people she may not seem to exist, but this day, this hour, this moment, she existed to her God. Riley might be dead. She might never see him again in this lifetime. All that might be true, and it would make her sad, but nothing could diminish the joy she felt knowing the love of God in her life. She had been hungry and suffered with trials and tests, but her Lord had sent the quail, pheasant and birds of the air to feed her and protect her from the demons of despair. Just the other day, she had read how the ravens fed Elijah, and now birds were helping her. The storms had been troublesome, but the truth was she was never without water to drink or to use to make soup. Gratitude consumed her entire being and she felt she too could fly up and away from the trouble and chaos that had bound her to the life of loneliness and grief. She had pressed in and pressed through to that place of contentment and unspeakable joy that imprinted her spirit with fresh revelation. She was no longer just an earthly child who cared about what other people thought. She was no longer afraid of revealing the beauty of her singing voice to show her love to her Creator with all her heart, mind and strength. Ruth was a new creation. Out of her spirit came a song that she sang to her Creator:

There's a joy I feel within my spirit,
Makes me want to run and jump and sing,
Jesus freed me from all earthly bondage,
To you this gift He'll gladly bring.

I just want to praise and dance and worship.
Yes, that's all I ever want to do.
Jesus freed me from all earthly bondage,
Won't you come and worship with me, too.

Next she was inspired to make an earthly vessel to give to the Lord. Tears ran down her cheeks as she took her fingers and dug out some dense red clay. The ground she lived on was now holy ground to her. She allowed her tears to mingle with the clay that she molded with her hands. Her fingers began to bleed as she worked. Both the tears and blood worked into her creation. This was an offering given out of praise and gratitude to her God. It didn't take long for the vessel to dry in the hot sun. Ruth displayed a bouquet of wild purple cone flowers in her newly fashioned container. The Lord God of the universe was greatly pleased.

CHAPTER 5

BE SEEING YOU, IF ONLY IN MY DREAMS

Each night, prayers were sent up asking that Riley and Sadie would be kept safe and make it home. Each morning, a mark was placed by the last one to record the days she had been apart from them. As the marks increased, Ruth seemed to cry less often.

"Riley, it does not mean I don't miss you. But doggone it, darlin', I'm just about cried out. I got the same ol' achin' in my heart for you. It's just that my eyes seem to be dryin' up. That is what I wish those ol' creeks and rivers would do so Sadie could bring you home to me. You and me, we got to do a lot of talkin'. I know, yes, I know, all you want to do is kiss and you know what...but Riley, I don't know hardly anythin' about you. Well, except that I love you and find you handsome and fun. Hum, let me think here. What do I know about you?"

Ruth leaned back on her mat with her fingers laced behind her head and stared up to the ceiling as she visualized the first time she ever saw Riley.

* * * * *

The sun was shining on the right side of him and his buckskin as he came riding down from Bowie, Texas. When he arrived at Adela's backyard, he slowed to a trot, then slowly reined the horse to a complete stop. His dismount was smooth, almost graceful. Tying the reins to the trunk of a cottonwood, he then patted his horse and spoke something into his ear. The horse stood there content, nibbling on the Kentucky ryegrass. First thing Ruth noticed was his horse and how he handled him, and then she noticed his hat. This was a wedding he was coming to and he wore his workin' hat. Next, she noticed his clothing. They were neat and clean but they looked like his workin' clothes. As she watched, he pulled something out of his saddlebag. It was wrapped in gingham cloth. He tucked the satchel under his arm. Looking around at the scene, he started toward the guests, who were already finding their seats lined up in rows facing an altar covered with red roses and a white washed home-made arbor.

The groom, Matthew, emerged from the crowd and swiftly walked toward him, extending his hand to welcome. Ruth couldn't hear a word they said. However, both looked happy to see each other, and their antics were like two young boys full of life and mischief.

Adela had confided in Ruth that there was a fellow coming to the wedding that she wanted her to meet. Riley was his name, but Matt called him Rye, as a nickname he and his other friends called him. Adela couldn't remember his last name, but Matt thought the world of him. All she knew was they had met and become good friends sometime ago in Kansas City, Missouri. At a carnival, those two country boys had eaten their first candied apple and rode on a Ferris Wheel. Together they had their picture taken, and both had kept a copy. Adela told Ruth that Matt had written Rye an invitation to the wedding in his own hand. That was how much he wanted Rye to come and share in their happy occasion.

Ruth just knew this must be that man Adela had told her about. She moved through the crowd of friends and relatives who were already beginning to sweat in their fine clothes. It was hot, all right. The circadian bugs were singing their own "Hallelujah" chorus when the fiddle player began to drown them out with his wedding music. This was the signal that it was time for Ruth to walk down the aisle leading to the out-of-doors altar. When she arrived at the front, standing to the right of the pastor, she looked around and caught a glimpse of Riley sitting on the back row closest to where he tied up his horse. She still couldn't get a good look at his face, even with his hat off.

The music changed and all the guests rose to their feet as Adela appeared covered from head to toe in white lace and a full-length, pearl-adorned veil. She walked nervously, clinging to her father's arm. Her mother was already drowning out the music with her wailing and carrying on. Ruth straightened out the train of Adela's wedding gown and held the bride's bouquet, while Matt and Adela joined hands and pledged their love to God and to each other so all the guests could hear.

Ruth turned her head as her eyes roamed the back row to see if Riley was still where she last saw him. He was. Riley was looking with a great big smile on his face. It almost looked like he rubbed a tear from his eye. This distraction almost made her miss her cue to hand the bouquet back to the bride as the couple were introduced as Mr. and Mrs. MacCleod.

Once they were down the aisle, a near stampede was made to the three tables laden with wedding food. Every dish imaginable was displayed on those fancy decorated tables.

The fiddle player changed the music and joined the other musicians. The party began.

Old folks were lined up kissing and blessing the newlyweds, while kids of all ages were sneaking tastes of the wedding cake frosting. Men gathered in their circles, taking off their ties and coats that grew hotter by the minute. The atmosphere was charged with joking, laughing and generally enjoying family and friends who had traveled far distances for this special wedding. Likewise, the women gathered in their circle, and much of the conversation included trying to guess what was inside the wedding gifts. Next to the surplus food, the wedding presents were piled high on the back porch just waiting to be opened. Ruth's brother and some of his friends sneaked off to the side of the house. Ruth saw a bottle being passed around.

Adela and her father had the first dance, and then he reluctantly handed her over to Matt so they could dance their first dance as husband and wife. Ruth was afraid the menfolk were going to have to carry Adela's mother out; she was crying and carrying on again.

People started coupling up and dancing. That's when Riley showed up. He edged up as close as anybody could without touching Ruth.

"Hello there, pretty lady. Would you honor me with a dance?"

Ruth jumped with surprise and then looked up at his handsome face with a smile meant only for her. She didn't remember if she said anything to him She just took the hand offered to her, and together they walked to the dancing area.

Ruth's heart was pounding so much she could hardly hear the loud music. Her throat went dry. It seemed all her moisture went to her hands. Riley didn't seem to notice. He pulled her close to him as the music soared to the "Cotton Eye Joe." He was a better dancer than her. It didn't matter because he held her tight and seemed to carry her around the dance floor.

He smelled clean of shaving soap and manly, as only hard working men smell. His eyes were as blue as robin eggs and his hair the color of wheat right before harvest. His fair complexion was taut like only sun and wind can make it. He had a full proud mouth that was singing the lyrics into her ear. Her neck felt the warmth of his breath, which gave her a feeling inside she had never felt before. It felt good.

They danced until the musicians took a break, and then together they searched out the punch bowl. Adela and Matt came up and made the unnecessary introductions. They had been opening wedding presents while Riley and Ruth had been falling in love on the dance floor. Matt came to thank Riley for the hand-carved Swiss-designed wooden clock that would find a special place in their new home. He also came to steal a dance from Ruth. As they danced he wanted to ask what she thought of his friend. He didn't need to ask. Ruth kept her eyes on Riley the whole time he was dancing with Adela. Matt also noticed Riley was not talking to his bride. Instead, he was looking back at Ruth the whole time she was dancing with him.

When that dance was over, Riley and Ruth reunited and went to the food table.

Half of a steer had been roasting in a pit for two days and then sliced thin and covered in barbecue sauce. On the same table was a plump stuffed turkey next to fluffy mashed potatoes and country cream gravy. There were so many vegetable dishes fresh from family gardens that the excess had to be stored on the back porch. An entire table was filled to overflowing with fried okra, squash, tomatoes, roasted ears of corn with hand-churned butter, light bread, as well as three kinds of cornbread, fresh string beans cooked with new potatoes and ham hocks. These were placed next to the green onions and last autumn's chow-chow relish, pickled baby beets, cucumber pickles-- both dill and sweet. Aunt Fanny brought her favorite fried green tomatoes that seemed to be the first to go. There were deviled eggs, coleslaw, collard greens, hot and sweet peppers, and it seemed every kind of pie and cookie known to man. Ruth and Riley piled their plates with samples of all the delicious morsels available.

The wedding cake deserved its own table. The three-tiered structure was a masterpiece of Lady Baltimore sweet cream vanilla cake with rich butter cream frosting. Because of the heat of the late afternoon, it was melting and dripping onto the table. The church ladies put in charge of the meal were fretting over the cake and insisted everyone stop their merriment to watch the newlyweds cut and eat their wedding cake. Each of the guests were given a glass of special Scottish wedding punch called Syllabub to toast the bride and groom. After it seemed like fifty or more long-winded toasts, everyone returned to eating, talking, dancing and laughing. The best quilts made for this occasion were spread under the shade trees so babies and grandpas could take a nap. Meanwhile, the younger folks danced, played horseshoes, ate cake and other desserts or entertained themselves playing blind man's bluff.

Riley managed to get some of everything on his plate. He sat across from Ruth, bowed his head and asked a blessing on his food. That gesture pleased Ruth. She was too fascinated watching Riley to touch anything on her loaded plate. She was more than a little amazed how he could eat as he did and still manage to breathe. For her, she had no appetite. He excited her so. He looked up from his empty plate and gave her one of his charming grins. Pointing with his fork he said,

"Are you goin' to eat that turkey there?"

Ruth smiled at him and shook her head no. She was more than glad to relinquish anything on her plate.

They sat there for a while and talked about the weather, the wedding and horses. Then they got up and danced until the sun went down and the moon came up. Matt and Adela's beautiful wedding was officially over when the bride threw her bouquet and Ruth caught it. The guests waved goodbye and threw rice to the happy couple as they rode off into the night in their "Just Married" decorated wagon.

Ruth's ma and pa assumed she would ride home with her brother. Ruth waited awkwardly until Riley asked her if he could walk her home. Those three miles never seemed so short.

Riley walked holding Ruth's hand. Buck, his horse, followed them like a puppy dog. They agreed they had never seen the full moon so big nor an evening so pleasant in August. A cool breeze was a welcomed relief from the heat of the day. Together they noticed the lights were still on as they approached Ruth's house. They agreed it was too late for him to come in and meet her parents.

There at the foot of the porch, still holding hands, neither were sure what to do next. It was actually Buck, that got things started. He nudged Riley toward Ruth. They came so close their noses touched. Ruth boldly kissed him. Riley eagerly returned the kiss. No words could describe it. Ruth wanted more. They embraced until the sound of her pa broke them up.

"Ruthy, is that you out there? Say goodnight to that feller and come on in the house now."

Ruth did just that, said goodnight with no promise of ever seeing Riley again, except in her dreams.

CHAPTER 6

SURVIVING OR THRIVING?

There didn't seem to be any dreaming tonight. The wind blew, making that deafening howling sound that caused Ruth's head to throb. The willow sticks were not working. It hurt so bad she vomited up the little soup she had eaten. Curled up in her covers, she prayed for sleep.

At first light, she was worn out. She had to get some sleep, she was starting to see things that weren't there. In her carpet bag was her old diary she brought from home but had not opened it the whole time she had been living in the dugout. With the quilt wrapped around her and the diary in her hand, she climbed up into the bed of the wagon. Ruth flipped through the pages to find a happy time recorded in her book. Straining her eyes in the early dawn she stopped at the entry dated: **Christmas 1897**

> **Dear Diary,**
>
> My birthday was the best. Ma made me a cake, and Pa brought in a box for me to open. It was my birthday present: a bit with reins. He motioned me to bring my new present and follow him to the barn. There in the first stall was a two year old Morgan horse. She was my Christmas present. There she stood with the saddle I picked out last summer at the stock show in Abilene, Texas. Pa was so proud. He put the bit in her mouth and lifted me up onto her. Ma was

**fretting about me getting cold and made me wear a
scarf on my head and her leather gloves and jacket.**

**James asked me what I was going to name her. I
knew right off: Sadie. I'll name her Sadie Sue. I sat
on her, feet in the stirrups, hands tight on the reins.
Leaning over, I whispered in her ear,**

"Sadie Sue, I love you."

She stopped chewing her hay and listened.

**We walked around the corral until we got used
to each other. Yep, she was mine and I was hers. I
released my tight hold on the reins, then ever so
gently, I nudged her in the ribs, and off she trotted.
Before I knew it, she was running, and then next, we
were flying.**

James, Ma and Pa were whooping and hollering.

That was a happy day. It was the very first time her family acted
genuinely happy for her and trusted her with her very own horse.

James, being the eldest and a boy, seemed to be able to do anything
he wanted. Ma and Pa encouraged him to be brave and free, to take risks
and explore. It seemed all those desires slipped off of her brother onto
Ruth. She was the one who begged for a horse, but he was given riding
lessons. She always wanted to go riding without a saddle and help out
with the farm animals. James didn't care if he ever rode, and whenever
he did, he never thought about riding bareback. Ruth had watched her
pa and the ranch hands work horses: from helping with the birthing,
breaking, feeding and grooming. She wanted to do it all but was told she
was too little to ever be strong enough to work around horses. The horses
needed to know who was the boss, and she was told she would never get
the hang of it. What all those menfolk didn't know was sometimes Ruth
would sneak out of her bedroom at night, go to the barn, bridle a horse
and lead him to the corral. There she would climb the rail and jump on
the bareback horse. They would quietly walk away from the ranch house
and bunkhouse and then ride off into the night. Her cow dog, Buster,

would go with them and keep watch. Sometimes the guineas would start to squawk when she came out of the house, but she knew how to quiet the main hen, and the others would calm down as well. Never was she so free as when she was riding on the range by the light of the moon. Ruth always led the horse for a drink, and she would listen to all the sounds of the night. The crickets would serenade her with the fiddles on their feet. Frogs would blend their rhythmic croaking with the occasional splashing of a fish to the symphony of the night. Often, a cow would be mooing to her calf, or a lookout prairie dog would bark at them as they walked by him carefully to avoid stepping into one of the holes that entered his tunnel home.

The gentle breeze provided a welcomed temperature change from the exhausting heat of the day. It would whistle through the willow and cottonwood trees lining the creek. Lightning bugs made no sound but were a welcomed delight. Some of the grass was so tall it made a swishing sound as the horse waded through it to the creek. Ruth could feel that grass on her bare feet as the horse walked through, stopping from time to time to graze. June bugs had their own tones, and some birds were awake and singing. One of her favorites was an old hoot owl that would startle her. Even so, she felt privileged to hear him hoot from the hollow of the elm tree or hear him swoop through the sky in search of a field mouse or a grouse.

Buster had a keen sense of time and would bark to let the horse know it was time to turn around and head for home. Each horse she rode knew the way back to the barn and would run faster home than he had run to the creek. Once back at the barn, Ruth would slide off and brush the horse down before putting him back into his stall with a handful of oats to munch on before sleeping. Even back in her own bed, as she closed her eyes, Ruth was still galloping bareback through the night until she heard the shrill holler of her ma,

"BREAKFAST, GET UP YOU SLEEPY HEADS! *This is the day the Lord has made, we shall rejoice and be glad in it.*"

Ruth would jump out of bed and wash up, dress and run down to help her ma with breakfast.

Ruth chuckled at the memory.

"*I think James always knew my secret because he would sometimes look at me across the breakfast table with a funny little grin on his face. I'd just pretend I had no idea what he could possibly find so amusing so early in the morning. But, he knew, and as far as I know, he never told on me.*"

Ruth loved those late-night escapes to Arenumi's home. This was her haven where she could be herself with a friend that was a kindred spirit. A mind full of memories, she longed to see and talk to Arenumi again. She felt her spirit lift and seek her friend.

In her mind's eye, she was soon transported to a calm place, and the air smelled sweet of apple blossoms. Ruth looked down at her body and saw that she wore a loosely fitted white cotton dress, and she was barefoot. Ruth turned slowly around, taking in the greens, reds, golds and browns of the terrain. She could see her horse frolicking in the tall buffalo grass. Ruth whistled for Sadie. Obediently, she came and stood by the railing of the corral. Effortlessly, Ruth climbed the railing, and without saddle or reins, mounted her horse and galloped off. They were flying. She and Sadie were one, moving in harmony, free. Sadie slowed to a trot when they approached Arenumi's home. Holding onto the mane, Ruth swung her body down and greeted her friend at the door. Her friend's teeth were perfectly straight and white that were always noticeable in her welcoming smile.

"*Haa muh rah way ka. Nuh nah nee' ya sah, Arenumi, Nuh say Numunu.*"

"*Arenumi, hello! What did you just say to me in your language?*"

"*Ruth, I greeted you with a welcome and told you my name. You come to visit me, friend. Have you had food today?*"

"*If I had, I'd lie just to taste whatever smells so good.*"

"*Come. Sit.*"

Arenumi brought out hot grease bread and a plate of roasted corn ears. Ruth watched as Arenumi ladled out some steaming stew into a bowl and placed it in front of her. Arenumi thanked everything on the table and the Creator of it all. They both broke bread, using it to sop up the tasty broth. Arenumi listened as Ruth told her about her dugout and fighting the snake. Arenumi listened and smiled, nodding her head in approval. Ruth woke up with the sunshine peaking through the burlap curtains. The winds had stopped, and it looked like a beautiful day.

"*What a wonderful dream to wake up from and now be greeted with sunshine and no wind.*"

Mr. Lizard came running inside the dugout at the sound of her voice.

"*If you're not the best little friend. Even though you don't make me grease bread or stew, you are fun to have around. 'Uh Kah Muh Kuh Tuh Nuh'. Mr Lizard that is Arenumi's language for I love you.*"

Mr. Lizard ran to her so she could pet him.

"Let's see, what are we going to do today? I can read to you. Would you like that?" He turned facing the door.

"Or, we can go weed the garden and you can scare the spiders away."

That little horned lizard ran out the door, and then seeing the shadow of a hawk moving across the ground made him turn around and run right back inside. Ruth had been watching this little drama and stuck her head out of the dugout, curious to see if it was her hawk. She shaded her eyes with her left hand and looked up into the cloudless blue sky. Her red-tailed hawk, Helper was riding the thermals.

"You make that look fun."

She heard the hawk squeal as if answering. Ruth ran out of her house with her arms stretched out like wings, jumping up in the air, halfway believing she would take off and soar through the sky. In this one moment she felt free She was free.

"I like this feeling. I think I'll keep it." She smiled, remembering Arenumi's smile. Her friend knew this feeling. Why else would she smile so easily? Again, her attention was on the shadow cast from the soaring hawk. She watched as Helper, her hawk, would circle and then take off to the north. She would come back, circle and then soar again in the northerly direction.

"Are you trying to tell me something? That's it, you want me to go see what you are pointing out to me. Maybe I should go back and get my gun... Oh, I'll just trust you since you bring me pheasant."

Stretching out her arms again, she ran as if she was flying high in the sky while following her aerial scout. Helper squealed a warning to her when she was almost to the edge of the arroyo. It was too late. Her foot slide on the loose dirt, and then her whole body began sliding on the rough gravel. There at the foot of the arroyo's sloping wall was a dead coyote. It was the biggest coyote she had ever seen.

"Maybe it's not a coyote, could it be a wolf? Hum, I don't remember my uncle Wilbur every saying there were any wolves in this area, and if so, they usually travel in packs."

She looked all around to see if there might be a small cave in the side of the gully. What was normally a dry gully had become a rivulet due to all the rain. This animal looked like it had washed up. Some sticks and pieces of tree limbs had washed up with the wolf. Taking one of the sticks, she poked it to make sure it was really dead. Upon further examination, this wolf had been shot, leaving a big exit wound in the shoulder.

"Look at you, you poor thing, you couldn't walk. Your front leg was almost shot off. Where did you come from, anyway?"

Ruth looked at this pitiful carcass and only thought of one thing: fur. Up in the sky, the hawk was long gone. All that was flying were the female flies ready to lay their eggs, nature's clean-up crew.

"Thank you, anyway, my darlin' feathered friend. I will make use of this fur before the maggots or ants steal it from me."

She clawed her way up the bank and stuck her stick as a marker so she could find this place again. Once she had retrieved her knife from the dugout and got her gun, she would return prepared in case other four legged furry things might come looking for their brother or come looking to eat it. With all this on her mind, Ruth ran back to the dugout, stopping from time to time to mark her path, leaving a trail back to the wolf and his wonderful pelt.

She methodically skinned the wolf, leaving the head and carcass where it lay and carried the pelt back to the wagon bed to further clean the hide. Mr. Lizard was eager to observe the whole thing. Ruth used her instructional voice when she spoke to her pet.

"Arenumi told me that her people would put pee on the skins to tan the hide. She said to scrape all the flesh off, stretch it out with the hide facing the sun, and then put pee on it. Finally, salt it so it would dry faster. All right, I guess I have to use what I have. That fur will come in handy this winter. As much as all this sickens me, I'll do it. People have been doing these kind of things for centuries. It's all natural. God made people to eat food, drink water, and pee. I can do this. Hum, this would be easier if I was a man."

Mr. Lizard was at her feet looking up at her turning his googly eyes every which way.

"Well, if I am embarrassing you, then look with those goofy eyes of yours in a different direction." He ran over and stood close to one of the buckets.

"Oh, I see what you're thinking. Thank you, my dear, you have saved me my dignity. I'll just use this bucket for a few days and collect enough to do a good job on the pelt. You are a genius, Mr. Lizard. I never knew reptiles could be so smart."

The horned lizard closed his eyes and, with a contented smile, sat motionless soaking up the warmth of the sun. Ruth stretched the hide in the bed of the wagon and carefully scraped off the remaining flesh from the carcass. All that remained was left for the flies, ants and other scavengers that roamed the prairie.

After salting the hide, she noticed she had used more than half in the pouch.

"Did I put salt on that list I gave Riley? I can't remember. I sure hope I did."

Ruth examined her work and was pleased how evenly she had removed the flesh, exposing a cream-colored hide to begin the tanning process. She had done this before on a smaller scale when she skinned the rabbits and even the pheasants, but this time she was not prepared for her hands to hurt so much. She washed her hands with her precious soap and then rubbed them with some fat she had saved from the wolf's hide. The oil cloth had done a good job keeping the ants out or was it her friend, Mr. Lizard, who protected her food from being ravished by the ant world? He was good at keeping away the spiders, beetles, flies and centipedes as well.

"I never thought I would love a lizard. Shoot, I never thought I would ever tan a hide, kill a snake, or any of this. I never thought I could live alone out here, but I guess Riley is right, I'm not alone."

Ruth had put in a good day's work and decided to go inside and take a nap. It was considerably cooler inside the dugout.

"I'll be, this place is either blowing so hard you can't think or it is so hot and still there's not a breath of air anywhere."

She wrapped her greasy hands in some strips off her petticoat. She kept ripping pieces off for the needed fabric, and now the undergarment didn't even cover her knees. Leaning back on her quilt, Ruth looked up at the ceiling and thought about petticoats and clothes. These thoughts triggered other thoughts of her friend, Adela.

"I think, Adela, your mama made you the prettiest clothes. Even if you were out chopping cotton, you had a dress on with pretty flowers covered with an eyelet apron. Oh, Adela, I don't know where your mama found the lace for your wedding dress. Everyone just thought you were lovely. I always dreamed of getting married and having a white wedding dress, a veil and a bouquet of flowers. That picture in the book of Granny's wedding dress made her look like a fairy princess. Riley and I just had our traveling clothes on when that circuit-riding preacher married us."

Ruth continued to think about how much fun she had at her cousin Matt and her friend Adela's wedding. Ruth's ma had altered one of her own nice dresses for Ruth to wear as Adela's Maid of Honor. Ruth had flowers woven together in a circle to crown her head. It was a smaller version of the bride's headpiece that attached to the long flowing veil.

Friends and relatives made all kinds of gifts to give to the newlyweds. Matt had an enormous family living in the Possum Kingdom area, and they were much wealthier than her family. Adela's folks gave her quilts, embroidered linens, towels, canned fruit and jellies, sewing supplies and a pretty nightgown for the wedding night. Matt's family gave them silverware, china and glassware, a fine Arabian horse; and a two-year-old milk cow.

Adela was now Mrs. Matthew MacCleod. She was living with her in-laws until Matt and his pa could finish the house on the land given to them by his grandpa, Ol' Silas MacCleod.

Matt had told Adela and she had told Ruth an interesting tale about their kin folks. The way the story went was like this:

Silas MacCleod, from Edinburgh, Scotland, was sweet on a lass named Sally Cockburn. Sally Cockburn was Granny Stewart's maiden name. She and her family were part of a displaced clan from the countryside surrounding the castle in Edinburgh, Scotland.

Sally did not share the feelings of affection toward Silas as he did for her. She rejected him and married a handsome brute named William Stewart. Silas, William, Sally and infant John all arrived from Scotland on the same boat to America. The irony of all of this history was John Stewart, William and Sally's son married Silas's daughter, Molly MacCleod. So now it seemed, they were all family and they all lived in Texas.

Both men came to America with one gold coin in their pocket. Granny had told Ruth that Ol' man MacCleod still had his Scottish coin and the very same pants he wore while traveling to Texas. Granny had brought with her, from the old country, ancient Scottish gold coins. It was her treasure. It may have been some of the Roman gold the soldiers had brought with them in their conquest of Caledonia. This treasure Granny secretly gave Ruth on her sixteenth birthday to use as her dowry. The worth of it, she had no idea. Granny said it would buy many good horses and even pay for the building of a nice wooden house and barn. It was just Granny Stewart's and Ruth's secret, Riley didn't even know about it. It was like the planting seed, not to be wasted.

"Riley doesn't know about it, Lord. I'll tell him when he comes home. If I had told him when we first met I wouldn't have been sure he loved me for me and not just to get my gold. God, forgive me. I know I shouldn't keep secrets from my husband, but just think how surprised he will be when I do tell him. It'll help make our dreams come true. When I met him at Adela's

wedding, he liked me for me. Then when he came back and found me at the arbor meeting, he still liked me. All the boys I knew were like my brother. They never liked me, heck they never even talked to me or looked at me."

Ruth rolled over on her mat, hugged the rabbit fur pillow and thought about Riley.

"Oh, my love, did you ever guess such a scrawny woman could have such a big heart full of love for you? I think I loved you when you came over after the wedding and asked me to dance. You held me in your arms and you pressed me close to your body as you swept me around the dance floor. You had a clean manly smell and even though your hands were rough, they held my hands tenderly. Your touch made me feel feelings I never felt before, and thinking of you makes me feel them all over again. I remember I could feel your breath on my neck, and our lips came so close we almost kissed. I wanted you to kiss me. That's why I let you kiss me when you walked me home. Well, if it weren't for your horse, I really kissed you first. You wanted to kiss me all night, but I was scared. Riley Earl, I'm not scared anymore, and when you come home to me, I will kiss you and love you all night long, if you want me to."

Ruth's next memory was not so pleasant and she felt her face get hot as she relived the shame and anger of that event. After all, Riley was a proper gentleman. He came to see her after the cattle drive. He had money and could now ask Pa for her hand in marriage. There was a "Sing" as they called it, and people from miles around came to sing, hear preachin' and, of course, to eat. Every family was to bring food to share and a pie or cake to be sold to raise money for the missionary fund.

"Lord, You know I did my very best to make that peach pie. The crust got a little too brown, but the rest of it was just fine. I had sprinkled some nutmeg in it, and that was the first thing that Ma complained about. It was too expensive to be wasting on a pie I was going to give away. Then she looked at it and told me it was not fit to throw to the hogs.

Ma, Riley paid $5 to buy my pie. That was the most anyone paid for a pie to give to the missionary fund. None of the other girls at church sold their pies for that much money. He ate the whole pie, but he did give me a taste. It was good, and I'll get even better with practice. But Ma and Pa, you two had to get ugly in front of all those church folks and shoo him like he was some kind of bug pestering me. Oh, you are so clannish. Proud Scots you are. Well, I'm a proud Scot, but that doesn't mean I need to shun anyone who's not!

You couldn't run him off without me, and I'm glad. He is brave and he is a good man and, doggonit, I love that man. Yes sir, I love him. And

*wherever he is right now, he knows I love him and he loves me, and he better
not be looking at any other women or eatin' their pies."*

Ruth was all worked up and upset. She got the bucket and went
outside. There were black clouds gathering in the southwest sky. Ruth
breathed out a big sigh.

"Yep, another storm is coming. I better take in that hide."

CHAPTER 7

RUTH REDEFINED

Sometime in the middle of the night, Ruth awoke to the sound of thunder. It was not raining. She stood at the door of the dugout and watched as the lightning sliced through the black sky, flashing such light that for an instant she could see clearly the out-of-doors. The thunder came quickly behind the light in such force Ruth could feel the rumble within her heart. More lightning, then more pounding thunder, like an awakened drum beating within every cell in her body. The force of this mystical energy caused the hair on her head to stick out as well as the hair on her arms. The next crash of thunder was so loud it caused Ruth to experience temporary deafness. Some primeval force within her rose to match the external storm. Barefoot and only with tattered petticoat on, she stepped out of the shelter into flashing, crashing space. The force was all around her. Red flames leaped up in the distance after the lightning in the sky reached its skeleton fingers to touch the ground. The fire grew as prairie grass was consumed by the red, orange, yellow and blue of the fire with its greedy tongue lapping up the rain-drenched land. Deep rumbling shook the earth. Her feet obeyed her body and moved to the frenzy of the storm. Ruth lifted her arms into the air as a gesture of surrender, reaching with her hands to touch the face of God. Her dance increased with speed into its frantic music, transporting her to that timeless place where all must go to be at one with the universe. Ruth danced even as the angry storm dissolved into tears which fell down from the heavens to the earth, soaking all it touched and transforming the hot prairie fire into cool black smoke. Only the rhythmic song of the frogs remained as Ruth's crazed dance continued. Finally the storm moved on to sleep in another sky and, in its passing, gave way to the cascades of sun rays drinking up the chaos of the night. Feeling drained from thoughts of gloom she had managed to dance away, Ruth's internal storm also fell asleep, as she collapsed wet on the bed of the wagon. She awoke sometime later, dry and refreshed. Ruth thought she had never felt so clean.

The sun was straight overhead. Ruth was still in her wagon soaking up the warmth. She was the most rested she had ever felt and decided to climb down and go inside to get dressed and bring out the hide. She checked her garden and then the buckets that were full of fresh rain water. She kept that one bucket inside, which she used to collect her special hide tanning solution. As she unrolled the wolf hide and put it out to dry in the back of the wagon, she kept hearing a buzzing sound. Curious, she followed the sound away from the wagon to the plum bushes. The bees were working the heavy blooms and dancing off in the direction of the creek.

"Lord, am I going to get some honey today?"

Thrilled with the prospect, she ran back to the dugout and grabbed her only bowl and a knife.

"I'm just going to join you honey makers in your dance and partake in some of your sweet labor."

Her ears did the work in directing her right to the stump of a fallen tree that appeared to have been knocked down and burned inside.

"Probably struck by lightning," she thought.

The bees were thick as she stood back and observed the scene.

"Lord, I've never robbed a beehive. I'm willing to do it! You know, I've been bitten or stung by almost all of Your other lovely little insects and almost by that delicious rattlesnake. Please Lord, show me how to do it so I don't ruin their honeycomb masterpiece. I really don't want to get stung either."

She sat there for the longest time just watching and waiting; for what, she didn't know. Without any thought or plan, she stood up, walked over to the hive and stuck her hand inside, then felt the sticky ooze. Pulling her hand out, she placed a piece of honeycomb in the bowl. She left the hive and walked a short distance and then turned around and thanked the busy bees for sharing. Although she felt like running or skipping all the way home, she was distracted by another sound. It sounded like a cow. Could it be a cow? She decided to take her prize back to the dugout and then explore this other sound.

"Mr. Lizard, I need you to guard this honey so those devil ants don't get into it."

Ruth licked her finger clean. Her mouth was so unaccustomed to this much sweetness she almost drooled on herself.

"Oh my goodness, Mr. Lizard is there anything better than this sweet honey?"

A sobering thought invaded her glee. Yes, Riley's kisses and loving were better and more satisfying. Dismissing those thoughts, she continued with her chore. She ripped off a piece of her petty coat and covered the bowl. She then found a rock larger that the bowl and placed it carefully over the cloth. Knowing her treasure was secure, she turned her attention to the cow sound. Out the door, up the knoll and down to the creek she raced to investigate the mystery.

The mooing cries were louder and were definitely a cow bawling in distress. This alarming noise forced her to run faster. Ruth almost slipped on the wet grass when she stopped at the top of the knoll and looked down at the creek. There they were; a cow and a calf. The mama had her horns tangled in some debris washed down by the creek during the rainstorm. The poor cow was halfway covered in mud, and the darling little calf stood helplessly by his distressed mother.

"Wow Lord. This really is the land of milk and honey. Now what? I have no idea how to free her from this miserable predicament."

Ruth took a deep breath, calmed herself, then assessed the surroundings. She'd have to wade through the water to reach the cow and calf, free her and then coax them both back through the creek and take them home with her.

"I guess if you can help me charm bees, you can help me rescue cows."

Her thoughts were interrupted by the cry of a hawk overhead. The sun blinded Ruth as she looked up. Shielding her eyes with her hand, she watched her hawk, Helper, as she landed on another fallen tree trunk that formed a small dam. That was the way Ruth would get to the cow and her calf and not have to wade waist-deep through the creek. The cow was looking at her with eyes that pleaded for help.

"Sweet Mama cow, I am going to free you and take you and your baby home with me. We can take care of one another. You'd like that, wouldn't you? Don't fight so much. You'll just get more tangled in the branches. I'm coming to get you."

She made her words soft, comforting, and musical so she'd not alarm the cow and further frighten her. In just a few long jumps, Ruth was on the other side of the creek and assessing the real problem. The long rope around the cow's neck was looped through a snag on a tree branch. She reached down and pulled the rope and the cow was free. She looked at the cow and saw that this was not the main source of her agony. Her bag was so full of milk it was about to burst. Right there, Ruth bent down and milked her enough so that the calf could get a tit in his mouth and suck. This beautiful Jersey cow now mooed with contentment, and her eyes said thank you to Ruth. After the calf had had enough, Ruth took the long rope and guided the mama and baby back to the dugout. She attached the end of the rope to a dead tree stump surrounded by tall grass. The calf laid down next to his mama and took a nap.

"I'm wore out too." Ruth confessed to the cows.

She joined her new companions in the cool grass and slept for a couple of hours. After her nap, Ruth went into the dugout and brought out her Bible to read out loud to the cows.

"You are my two new creatures to share the gospel with right now."

The mama lifted her head from grazing and listened to Ruth for a moment before returning to the grass.

Ruth braided some wild flowers into a fairy crown and placed it on the cow's head between her horns. Then she walked over and snatched a handful of weeds from her garden and threw them into the taller grass outside the rock border. The beet greens looked big enough to harvest, so she picked a few to add to her evening soup. When she entered the dugout, she returned her Bible to its safe, dry place, and she dropped down on her bed to rest from the heat of the afternoon. Ruth missed her supper because she slept without dreaming all through the afternoon and evening. She awoke just before dawn.

Ruth just stayed in bed, staring up at the ceiling, thinking of all the ways to use the milk and honey. Her breakfast was going to be a little ground corn cooked in milk, and topped with honey. Her stomach growled thinking about it. The sun was barely showing when she rose and dressed. Outside she heard a horse whine and her heart jumped into her throat.

"Riley!" she thought.

But instead she heard a stranger's voice.

"Hey there, is anybody to home?"

Fear now resided where excitement had lived. She grabbed the pistol and discovered Riley had not loaded the gun. There with the gun were all the bullets but none in the cylinder.

"Hey, come out and greet me, if anyone is home!" The voice was stern.

Ruth didn't have time to load the gun. Keeping it behind her back, concealed in her skirt, she emerged from the dugout. The sun was behind the mounted silhouette of the stranger, and she had to shield her eyes with her free hand to even see him.

"I see you found my cow and calf." He was loud and abrupt.

"Stranger, looks like she found me."

"I want her back."

"Don't see no brand on her."

"Oh, I see how it is. You can have her for eight dollars."

"That's more than what I'm willing to pay for a cow and calf."

"Young lady, I could just knock you down with my breath and take that Jersey, calf, and your money."

Ruth pulled out the gun and pointed it right at his heart. She was praying the bluff would work.

"I can shoot this gun. Keep the cow, my money, and your horse."

"Whoa now! I'm too God-fearing to be taking advantage of a half-starved girl! Where's your pa?"

"That, mister, is none of your concern. My husband is down by the creek. He hears this gun go off and he'll come a running."

"No, no. I don't want any trouble."

He slowly eased his horse back a few steps.

"Well then, I'll give you five dollars, four for the Mama and one for the calf. Deal?"

"Yes ma'am, it's a deal."

She ran back into the dugout, loaded the gun and took a coin out of a small pouch that held the Scottish gold coins her Granny had given her. Ruth grabbed a piece of paper and a marking tool. Stepping outside, she handed him the paper and the marking tool, still aiming at his chest, the now-loaded gun.

"Give me your mark and I'll give you the money."

"Oh, so we have a businesswoman here!"

He made his mark and received his gold coin. He looked over the gold and had a hunch it was worth more than a five dollar gold piece.

*"Where did **this** come from?"* He asked in amazement.

"From Scotland, and it spends the same anywhere in the world."

"Yes, ma'am it sure does." He tipped his hat to her,

"Well farewell, nice doing business with you."

She stood there with the gun pointed at him until he turned and rode out of sight. Weak and shaky, she leaned against the wagon and thanked God for His angel's protection.

"So he thought I was just some dumb girl. Well, I showed him. He learned I was a businesswoman and not afraid of him. I've got to mark my cow so people will know she belongs to me. I got a piece of paper, which may or may not mean anything, but I wanted him to know I knew what I was doing. Nobody is welcome to just come and take the things God has given me, nobody, not even the devil himself. This here land is Holy ground and my garden and livestock are consecrated, just like I am. He knows I'm a lady, too. I don't think he believed one minute my husband was about, but he didn't take advantage neither. He knew I was just scared enough to shot him in the heart. Oh Lord, thank you for sending me some big ol' angels to watch over me and protect me from evil. I don't want to have to shoot anything I can't eat. I sure do appreciate what all you've done for me this far. I'm still waiting patiently…all right, not so patiently- for Riley to come home to me. That would be the best gift of all. I do have faith for that miracle, I do, I really do."

She put the gun down and got two buckets. One of them she used to sit on and the other to hold the delicious rich creamy milk from the Jersey. As she leaned her head on the cow's side and listened to the rhythm of the milk squirt into the bucket, she began to hum a little ditty, and the cow swished her tail with approval. Leaving the calf to have his breakfast, she went inside to have hers. It had been thirty-five days since Riley had left to go huntin'. Tired of counting the days; she continued to count them, anyway. God, in his magnificent mercy, was caring for her in ways beyond her imagination.

"Oh Lord, Your ways are so much grander than my ways. I am so grateful. Everything You make is good. What adventure is in store for me today? Where was I just reading in the Bible? Oh yes, David and Goliath. That is one of my favorite stories."

Mr. Lizard came out of his hiding place licking his breakfast of ants off his mouth. He was ready to listen to his daily Bible story.

* * * * *

Ruth emerged from the dugout and moved the tether to another area of tall grass. The cow and the calf seemed content now. She bent down and began gathering dried cow patties to use as fuel and stacked them next

59

to the dugout. This blessing was to be her cash cow. She would now have cheese, butter, buttermilk, top cream, and fresh milk to drink. Cheese was her favorite food. Jersey cows were her favorite cows. Even though they were not big milk producers, they did produce lots of cream. When the plums ripened, she would dry some and store them up for the winter. Then, with the prairie chickens or maybe a plump pheasant, she could make Cock-A-Leakie, another popular soup her granny Stewart would make around the holidays. Those wild onions growing near the trees would be a nice substitute for leeks in the soup. Maybe next year she would plant some leeks in her garden so her recipe would be more authentic. The plan was to let some of the plants in her garden go to seed, and then she would save them to plant next year. Her wagon bed was the perfect place to dry out some vegetables and any meat Riley might be bring home.

"It will all work out and we will do just fine."

Her smile radiated new confidence, faith and hope.

The angry clouds of other nights had been swapped for a heaven full of stars. Big and yellow, the full moon lit up the countryside. Crickets were chirping and in the distance she could hear an old hooty owl preparing for his nightly hunt. The owls and hawks had kept the field mouse population away from her food and away from living in her dugout. There were still snakes, but she hadn't heard or seen anymore rattlesnakes. Mr. Lizard was getting fat on ants and spiders and the calf was growing daily on his mother's rich milk. Ruth was beginning to have more energy and those cracks on the sides of her mouth and tongue had disappeared since she was drinking milk. Her face seemed less fuzzy and the hair on her head was no longer falling out by the handfuls. Life was getting better. It would all be just perfect if she knew, for sure, Riley was coming home.

"I know my faith is being tested. Being brave is over-rated. Riley, I need you to come home. Where are you, darlin'? I'd come lookin' if I knew where to look. I feel as if a big ol' log is sticking in my heart, weighing me down."

Ruth hadn't had a good cry in a day or two; she was due one. With her face to the west, watching the crimsons and golds of the sunset, Ruth cried for Riley; craving his kisses and caresses. How had she lived this long without him? Her crying turned into sobs.

Ruth was lonesome and at moments like this, she felt she might just lose her mind if he didn't return to her. In an attempt to comfort herself, she tried to think of people she remembered and stories she had been told to get her thoughts off of missing Riley so much. Ruth willed her mind to float back to when she last saw Granny Stewart.

CHAPTER 8

LIVING IN A NEW REVELATION

Granny Steward sat on the porch that faced the sunset and filled her apron with some freshly picked string beans. She made her hands busy with the beans as she told Ruth a story about her family when they all lived in Scotland.

"My sweet girl, you may be little in stature and not have too much meat upon those bones of yours, and yet within the very blood that surges through that body of yours is a fierceness that cannot be denied. I am going to tell you a story that happened long ago that has changed our family. At first, this does not sound like a happy story or even a story worth remembering. No, it is a story of horror, of evil that was exceedingly bad. Even so, it is up to us that have lived on throughout the generations to make good out of what the Devil meant for harm. Bonnie Ruth, I want to be tellin' you about fierceness. Let my words sink into your bones: fierceness can be a strength, if used for what God calls to be good."

"This here is a true story if ever a told story be true. Your pa's great grandfather told me this story when I was carrying your pa inside my belly. The event happened to his great grandfather's family, him being one of the products of such a deed as told."

"The time of the year was in the spring, after the snow and ice had given way to the green growing things of this earth. It was the time of the planting moon. Out of the mist that hung upon the air, in the wee morning hours, a hoard of devils descended upon the village as it was sleeping. These demons had fire-colored hair on their heads and beards and their bodies were covered in animal skins. On their heads they wore helmets with the horns of oxen. They loomed a full head and shoulders taller than the Scots. First, they

sought out and killed all the able-bodied men, leaving the aged to live their remaining years in shame and the wee little boys to grow up fatherless. Each took to a cottage and rooted out the mutton and brew and then gathered together in the center of the village to make a huge fire. There, the brutes ate their fill and drank until they were drunk. All the women were frightened and some of them took their children and ran to hide. A few brave women sent their children to the glens while they stayed to fight the monsters. It did no good. The women who fled were found. Those fighters who stayed behind, lost their battle. All the women who were old enough to bleed were left with babies in their bellies when the savages left."

"Some of these women were so filled with grief from the murdering of their loving husbands and now being soiled by these invaders that they took their own life. Others clung to life and fixed their minds to thinking innocent babes could not be blamed or punished for what had happened. These women chose to live and repair the damage to their village and their hearts. It was not an easy task, for the crop of children produced resembled their fathers more than their Scottish mothers. Many had the red tint of hair. Most were large in height and girth. All were strong-willed and unruly. Every one of them loved to fight as much as they liked to eat. Whenever their mothers took the rod to them so as to punish them, these children, wee little lads or lassies, would wrestle the rod from her and break it. These children seemed brighter than their siblings, more clever in just about anything they took to task. Animals did not fear them. They seemed to come to them rather than run during the hunt. Their village was never without food. Even as wee children, they worked hard and accomplished much. Oh, but watch out for their tempers. Never, never anger one of them, or you would feel their wrath and feel it quickly. What was so odd, they were happy most of the time and showed it by laughing, singing, dancing and generally being merry. Not a stingy streak was in any of them, giving to anyone who seemed in need. That is until they became old enough to drink the brew. It was devil juice to their bodies. Mean they were. Raging and storming, leaving a wake of destruction wherever they went. When grown, some stayed and married. Most left to fight the wars. Of those who left, none came home."

"So you see, my dearest child, why your father is a mountain of a man. Hard to think that man, broader that an oak, came out of my body. He was no pleasure to birth, mind ya, but a sweet nature he had, nevertheless; that is, unless riled. You know your father's temper can only be matched by your mother's. Yes indeed, a marriage made in heaven, they are."

Granny looked at Ruth in the eyes and gave her half a smile after the last statement.

"Granny, you started this story telling me it could be a good thing to be fierce. When is it a good thing, Granny?"

"Oh, I don't know when it will happen, child. I just know it will someday and ya will remember my words. Ya will know. Trust me, darling, ya will be surprised that ya have it in ya. It's deep within ya; your blood holds it from long ago. God will use it for good, just be mindful that you don't use it for harm. Don't be fallin' into despair about anything in life, my love, your story is not over until the good Lord calls ya to Himself."

"Granny, I think I understand. Here, give me some of those beans and I'll help you get them ready for cookin'."

"Ya be a pleasure to me, Ruth. My child you are a true gift, and I can see a bit of red shining through that brown hair of yours, right here in this evening light."

Granny sat there silently lost in her own thoughts for what seemed a long while. She looked up and looked Ruth straight in the eyes and gave her a small smile.

"These beans will taste good tomorrow with that cured ham hock."

Granny Stewart stared off at the setting sun. Ruth watched her granny, both in silence, as they finished working the beans. Then Granny spoke, almost in a whisper.

"Ruth, you know why I told you that long-ago story about our kinfolk women who were hurt and shamed by those monsters of invaders? The way I see it, they came to the place in their heart where they just had to exchange hate for love. They decided to love those babies and not hate them. They also took the power away from that evil deed done to them by forgiving. That is what our Lord is trying to get us to choose every time something comes at us to shame us, or hurt us. It did not come easy, I know that to be true, but those women had to forgive and choose life instead of bitterness, which will make a person dead as can be even though they are still walking around in their own body. Ruth, I want you to remember what your ol' Granny is saying to you today. It doesn't make any kind of worldly sense to forgive, all I know is it works. I just want to obey the Lord God, even if I'm not wanting to at first. The Lord knows best and if He says do it, then do it."

That same ol' sun, of long ago, was setting again, still leaving the incredible crimson clouds streaking its evening blue sky. Ruth looked at the blooms on her bean plants and savored the memory of her Granny's words. Fierceness had served her well when the snake struck. She did not faint with fright. Each time a storm came bringing with it chaos, she endured it, then cleaned up after it. Whenever the stranger came to threaten to take the cow and calf, she claimed them but then did what was right by paying the man. She had not shot that stranger, although there was no doubt in her mind now that she could've. In all these things, she didn't have the strength or presence of mind to do any or all of these things. Something had changed in her, and mostly, it was the awareness that her mind was being changed. Ruth thought of herself differently and trusted the Lord for the first time in her life. Because of this new attitude, she just could no longer stay angry at her family and friends back home. She loved them all and couldn't feel hate, disappointment, or rejection anymore toward them or from them.

"Lord! Oh dear Lord, I forgive 'em. Oh, please please forgive me for taking so long to forgive them."

CHAPTER 9

LIVING LIFE AS A TRUE ADVENTURE

The cornstalks were getting tall. She was going to have a mess of English peas to eat and, maybe tomorrow or the next, a few squash and some green beans. The pintos were growing nicely. Large okra blossoms were open and the bees were delighted. The cabbage was just going to head. Three kinds of peppers were plentiful but not quite ripe; the onions seemed small; most of the beets and turnips had nice foliage. The parsnips and carrots weren't doing so well. They seemed to be all top with not enough root growing. What did she expect? She had planted everything at the same time and Granny Stewart believed God put signs in the heavenly bodies to use for planting. Granny planted using her folktale method and always talked to each plant and thanked them for being so delicious. This was her way of doing things, loving life and she always had a plentiful garden. Most years, she had to give vegetables away. Ruth laughed at the time she remembered being eight years old when Granny and she chased a cottontail rabbit that was eating Granny's cabbage. They caught it with a pillow case they took off of the line of clothes that was hanging with the rest of the laundry. It was the first time she ever heard a rabbit cry. It almost made her decide not to eat that little critter. However, that was the time in her life when she ate her fill at every meal and had not yet learned the harsh reality of the food chain. Her granny was a peace-loving woman and taught Ruth the great difference between killing and murder.

"Listen here, Ruthy. God put mankind in charge of all His creation. This is an important task. There is no mistake He named our family Stewart, 'cause He taught us to be good stewards of this precious world. Whenever *you harvest a crop or an animal, you only do so for nourishment or to trade off so others may have nourishment. You don't just kill anything out of anger or malice, that is murder, not killing. In wartime or for self protection, now that's another story. You better be sure you are prayed up for both because God doesn't just let you murder, even in wartime. You and I and the rest of the human race don't have enough sense to know who is really good or bad, so let God's spirit decide. Believe you me, God will let you know what you are to do in this matter. Yes darlin', He will, every time, if you ask. It's best you ask Him about everything in life. He smiles on you more and extends His hand of blessing to those of His children who honor Him and show good manners. Now another thing: be respectful and always ask using please, and show your gratitude by giving Him your thanks. Remember child, God wants good for you. He is funny that way with His children. Oh my, my, I love Him so!"* Reflecting on this memory, Ruth spoke out to her dearly departed Granny.

"Granny, I love the Lord, too. He is so good to me. You kept telling all of us how good He is even after all the hardship you faced. I think I understand you a little better now, Granny, now that I've been out here with God for these last forty days. I'm grateful you taught me even when you didn't think I was listening. You see, some of it soaked into my thick skull."

She looked out over the prairie. In midsummer, it would normally be hot and dry, but right now the land was green and colorful with patches of red, yellow, pink, and purple created by colonies of wild flowers. Birds singing, insects buzzing and the sound of her heart beating created a song played in nature's springtime orchestra. The earth and sky were brimming with life. All being temporal, it didn't matter. Mr. Lizard was happy sitting with his eyes closed. His face pointed into the sun. Elsie was lazily chewing her cud watching her calf, Elmer, frolic in the tall grass. Ruth opened her arms and reached toward the sky to embrace it all, absorbing the joy of the moment. She was at peace.

The creek was down to its normal size and the water was running clear when she took the cows for a drink and to get herself a fresh bucket of water.

"James, I wish you were here to catch me a fish for supper. I'm almost positive there are at least one or two catfish in that creek and there is probably some crayfish you could catch with your bare hands."

Her brother had noodled for fish but she never had. There were definitely fish in the creek. She would wait a couple of days before she tried fishing.

"Maybe I can catch fish with a pillow case just like Granny and I did with the rabbit." That was a good thought, since she didn't want to get fish bit, like catfish were known to do.

Elsie was taking a long drink and Elmer was playing in the water. Ruth was weaving a little basket with some of the reeds that grew next to the creek, since her last one had broken from the weight of the unshelled pecans. The squirrels were out again and chose not to bother talking to their pecan-stealing enemy.

"This might be a good day to bathe," she told the calf. The creek didn't have any strange debris flowing down it like after the storms and she would stay clear of the heavy reeds, where water moccasins liked to hide. Ruth looked around for a good place to hang her dress. She stuck her big toe in the creek to test the water. It was perfect, so she waded on in and dipped her head under and opened her eyes. She searched for a lazy catfish or any other life before surfacing for air. The water felt refreshing as her skin drank in the moisture. Rolling over on her back she floated and felt the hot sun caress her face and shoulders. However, when she stood up and waded back to the bank, the gentle breeze hit her wet body and caused her to shiver.

"Mr. Wind, you are blowing from the north today. No more storms for a while, please. I wonder what Riley is doing right now."

Quickly she dressed and headed back to the dugout, leading her cow friends close behind. Up over the little knoll she spied a man on horseback riding fast and whooping and hollering. Behind him was a pack mule. She heard her name being called. Ruth fell to her knees and began a hysterical mixture of laughing and weeping. It was Riley! No dream, no hallucination, and no phantom: it was Riley. Alive! Ruth tried to yell, but her voice would only make the sound of a whisper.

"He came home to me."

Ruth regained her footing and began to run. She pulled the long rope, and Elsie and Elmer ran behind her. She could tell from a distance that his saddle bags were bulging, and even better, behind him, a mule was fully loaded. Ruth's mouth went dry, and she was dizzy with excitement. She couldn't even feel the ground under her bare feet. All of a sudden she wondered what she looked like: hair and body wet and clothes loosely hanging around her thin body. Her shoes were in the dugout, but she didn't care about the stickers or the rocks. She was running so fast her feet were barely touching the ground.

Riley swung down off the saddle and in one movement lifted Ruth off her feet. Their kiss filled an eternity with passion. With their lips finally parted, they giggled like little kids, hugging and patting each other.

"Ruth, my love, you are here, you stayed, and you're here! Oh I've missed you and I love you, and I'm so sorry I couldn't get back to you. I know it has been forty days. Long old lonely days, but I'm here now. I had such trouble. The Red River flooded, and I couldn't get back."

He was talking a mile a minute but she didn't notice because of being in some sort of trance. She heard him and understood him, yet all she could focus on was that he was here. He'd come home. She could touch him, kiss him, hold him, and she had never loved him more than right now.

"Looky here, I brought us all kinds of grub; presents too. I killed a mule deer, but it was rainin' so much the meat was going to sour, so I traded it off, thinkin' I'd go huntin' some more when the dad-burn weather cleared. Instead, a rancher from Bowie, Texas took me in and let me work for him until the rivers and creeks dried up enough for me to get home to you. I had no way of gettin' word to you."

He stopped suddenly. He looked beyond the rope she was still holding.

"You got a cow? You got a cow and a calf? Where'd you get a cow?"

He was no longer looking at Ruth. He was mesmerized by the sight of the cow. He looked around at the dugout and beyond to the small stone wall surrounding the vegetable garden.

"Hey, and you got us a big ol' garden growin'?" He chuckled.

He shook his head and looked toward the heavens and mouthed the words,

"Thank you Lord!"

"Oh, see, it was a good thing you stayed here and took care of the place. You didn't have to endure all the hardships I had to go through, huntin' and worryin' myself sick tryin' to get back to you. Oh darlin', you look so beautiful, all clean and healthy. You are my best girl, my only girl."

He reached down and kissed her hard.

"I love you Ruth. I'm just so proud of you and so, doggone in love with ya!"

Ruth's head was spinning. Riley smiled at her and then began unloading the supplies of food; everything on the list and more. There was a new dress with flowers on it and four skeins of colored yarn with two sizes of knitting needles and a crochet hook. Riley had thought of everything: some dishes, new covers, good smelling soap and a can of tooth powder. He'd even bought two new tooth brushes with hog bristle made somewhere in Massachusetts. A large pouch of salt and a tin of black pepper was a surprise that was not on her list. Another surprise was a small pouch containing a nutmeg nut and a small metal grater.

"Thought we could always use more salt and pepper, as well as matches and some sweet stick candy. In that cloth with the candy is some bark that's called cinnamon. I just had to bring my sweetheart some candy. Sweets for the sweet, as someone once said. Now that we have a milk cow, you might be willing to make me a buttermilk pie. What do ya think darlin'?"

What she was really thinking was she had no oven to bake a buttermilk pie but she didn't want to ruin this glorious moment of homecoming, so instead she said,

"I am thinking you are wonderful," she whispered as he continued to show her all their treasured bounty. He hummed a happy little tune as he worked, clearly pleased with himself and his welcomed homecoming. Ruth walked over to him and put her hand on his shoulder.

"Riley, I have something to ask you."

"Yes, darlin', what is it?"

"While you were working for that rancher and gone from me so long"- she took a deep breath and let out a big sigh- *"did you get to sleep in a bed and did you eat fried chicken?"*

"Yes ma'am, and I brought with me in that cage loaded on the mule, two layin' hens and a mean ol' rooster. I can dress him for supper if you're hungry for chicken. You know I'd do anything for you."

His loving offer to please her opened up her heart, and all the pent-up anger she held for Riley leaving her alone for forty days seemed to vaporize and be gone. In place of that anger, a forgiving smile formed on her face.

"Oh, I know you would do anything for me, Riley. No sir, we'll be needing that ol' fella for more chickens. I just happen to have a pheasant in the house waiting to be roasted since my man is back home."

"Pheasant? You got me pheasant to eat? Oh wow, you are quite the lady. I feel rich. Yes, indeed, you are quite the lady."

Ruth hugged Riley and held him as tightly as she could.

Riley pulled away from Ruth with a start and put one hand on each of her shoulders and looked her square in the face and with a big grin said:

"Oh! Ruth, I have something real important for you."

Riley reached into his vest pocket and pulled out an envelope with Ruth's name on it. He looked at her quizzically as he handed it to her.

"There was a man named Wilbur. Never gave me his last name. He came to the ranch where I was working and waiting for the river water to get low enough so I could cross over and get back to you. I asked him how he knew you and how he knew to give this to me, but he never answered. He just smiled and tipped his hat to me, got back up on his horse, and rode off. It was sort of mysterious-like. Go ahead and read it while I unpack."

Ruth's hands were trembling as she carefully looked at her name on the envelope. She recognized her ma's handwriting. Carefully, she opened it so she wouldn't tear the paper and slipped out the letter. The confirmation was that this letter was handwritten on her ma's personal stationery. Ruth was already fighting back tears as she began reading.

> *"Our Beloved Ruth,*
>
> *If you are reading this letter then you are alive. Your pa and I have not given up finding you, darling. I know now **we** ran you off and we have prayed to the Lord that He would forgive us. Now we are asking if you and Riley will forgive us. You are our blood.*
>
> *Pa and our neighbors took out looking for you two and went to find where, in Texas the Welty's are living. He met up with Gilbert, Riley's brother. He is good people. They are just like us, trying to love God, family and work the land to make a living.*
>
> *Your pa has always been a headstrong Scot, but he is now changing into a new type of man. He is a Texan now. John Stewart is no longer stuck on only having his own way. His love for you is strong and true. He just never could tell you in words, but I got him to tell me. He is willing to try to tell you too if you will give him a chance. Well, if you will give both of us a chance.*
>
> *I see now I just never wanted you to grow up. My ma didn't want me to either, and I started hating her for the*

way she treated me. Then, lo and behold, I did the same thing to you. Ruth, I would give anything to have never thought those ugly thoughts that I spoke out to you.

Your brother and uncle gave us a talking-to. Your pa and I know they are right about you and Riley living your life the way you choose. Pa and I are living by the choices we make every day. Sometimes we have taken risks that our own parents thought were dead wrong. We made them anyway, not to disobey. We made our own choices because we knew they were right for us and within God's will. We understood it was our turn in life to do what we were birthed to do. Now, we reckon, it is your turn.

Ruth, you are a woman now. I promise to recognize it is true and not treat you like a child. I realize you cannot come back to the home you grew up in because you are making your own home with Riley. If the Lord blesses you with children, I sure would like to know them and love them.

Your pa and I are hoping you and Riley will come visit us sometime soon. If I knew where to send letters, I would like to write to you, and maybe you could write to Pa and me.

We miss you so much, our darling Ruth. Please, do not be mad at us anymore.

Ma and Pa

Ruth wiped the tears off her cheek and then carefully folded up the letter and put it back in the envelope.

"Ruth, darling, where in tar hill did you get a wolf? That is a great pelt you got there. What else have you got I don't know about? You have been one busy lady. Wow Wee!

As Riley was admiring the wolf pelt, Ruth noticed on the mule a satchel that was moving. She heard what sounded like a puppy whining. Riley was suddenly by her side, grinning from ear to ear.

"Yep, you best go over there and see what else I got ya. I'll put the letter of yours back in my pocket for safekeeping."

Ruth handed him the letter from her ma and then squealed like a little girl.

"Oh, Riley, how did you know? This puppy looks just like my old dog, Buster, when he was a pup."

By now, the little female puppy was in her arms, licking her face.

"Do you have a name for her? Maybe a sweet Scottish name? I thought I'd let you have the honor of naming the best huntin' dog in these parts. She's from a good pair of bird dogs and snake killers."

"Riley, I just love her. Oh but I love you more!"

Ruth gave Riley another hug and the puppy reached over and started licking his face.

"Little doggy, you need a special name. Your name is now Honey, 'cause your coat is as golden as that honey I've got inside the dugout that I robbed from the beehive down by the creek."

Riley looked at Ruth with surprise.

"I still can't believe all you got done while I was gone. I knew you were a good woman, and look at all this, and now you tell me you even found us some honey to eat? I'm so proud of you. Hot diggaddy, I married me a bee charmer, a real live bee charmer!"

Ruth put Honey down to explore her new home and she went straight for the bucket full of fresh water. Sadie neighed and Ruth walked over to pet her and remove the saddle and bridle.

"Don't be jealous, you know I've loved you the longest."

Sadie nuzzled Ruth with affection. They had a moment of loving reunion, and then Sadie went over and drank out of the same bucket where Honey had drunk. Ruth felt mighty fine and happier than she could ever remember. She took her skirt and lifted it up above her ankles and skipped over to Riley where he was unloading the mule. She whispered in his ear.

"And if those hens aren't laying for a day or so, due to their trip, I know where I can get us some quail eggs for breakfast."

He stopped what he was doing and reached over and took her in his arms. They held each other, looking all around and then into each other's eyes.

"Riley, you know what? We are rich. I have so much to tell you but right now let me cook that pheasant. I'm hungry, aren't you?"

There were no storm clouds in the sky that night, only a big ol' moon and a million stars.

RECIPES FOUND IN THE STORY FORTY DAYS WITH RUTH

Many recipes are lost in the mist of time or maybe the fairies stole them. Here are a few, some 250 years old, I found scratched on the backs of church bulletins, scrap paper and note cards. These are some of the foods my family ate while telling stories and swapping lies. These were the foods that came with the harsh instruction, "Take what you want but eat what you take." May you take what you want and enjoy and share with your family what you take. I feel confident that Ruth would be happy knowing that her family has enough to share with your family. So please accept this blessing from us to you,

"May our Father God bless you with health, wealth and a sense of mirth all the days of your life." Carol Welty Roper

BEVERAGES:

<u>SYLLABUB</u>

Also known as Atholl Pudding, a Scottish dessert drink used to toast the bride and groom at their wedding.

Ingredients:

2 cups heavy cream-whipped
½ cup whiskey or sweet wine (to make it non-alcoholic use ½ cup sparkling white grape juice)
¼ cup of fresh lemon juice with lemon zest
A pinch of ground cinnamon
½ teaspoon of almond extract
¼ cup of toasted pinhead oatmeal or 2 Tablespoons of toasted oat flour

Directions:

Chill large bowl and beaters and whip cold heavy cream to soft peaks. Add other ingredients and serve in wine glasses immediately.

<u>Author's notes:</u> This recipe serves about six people for a wedding toast. Other wines or champagnes may be used for more toasts but this drink is more of a traditional ceremonial drink. "Bub" is an English nickname for a drink with bubbles.

BREADS AND STARCHES:

<u>BANNOCKS</u>

Ingredients:

    3 cups all purpose flour or oat flour
    3 Tablespoons baking powder
    1 ¾ cup of warmed cow's milk
    ¼ cup melted butter or vegetable oil

Directions:

In a large bowl mix together flour, baking powder, milk and butter or oil. Stir until dough comes together in a ball; Do Not Over Mix, it does not have to be kneaded like other breads. Shape into rough oval; place on greased baking sheet. Bake until it becomes a beautiful golden brown color. Bake 400 degrees Fahrenheit for 30 minutes.

<u>Author's notes:</u> There are many recipes for bannocks, just like scones, soda bread or buttermilk biscuits. Bannocks are drier than these other quick breads due to less fat in the recipe. I like to remedy this by putting lots and lots of butter on them while they are hot and then lots of honey.

CORNBREAD

Ingredients:

1 cup all purpose flour
1/3 cup melted butter
1 cup yellow cornmeal
12 ounce can Mexican corn or whole kernel corn
4 teaspoons baking powder
½ teaspoon salt
1 egg, slightly beaten
1 cup milk
1/3 cup honey

Directions:

Combine dry ingredients. Add corn, toss lightly. Combine milk, butter, honey, and egg to dry ingredients. Mix until moistened. Spoon into lined or greased medium sized muffin tins, until 2/3 full. Bake 400 degrees Fahrenheit for 20 to 25 minutes Yield 18 Muffins.

FRY BREAD-COMANCHE/ APACHE

Ingredients:

4 cups all purpose flour
1 cup powdered milk
4 teaspoon baking powder
Warm water
1 teaspoon salt
Fat or oil for frying
1 cup lard or shortening

Directions:

Mix baking powder and salt into flour. With fingers work lard or shortening and flour together until it resembles corn meal in texture. Stir powdered milk into 1 cup of warm water and mix into the flour mixture to make a dough. Turn out on floured surface and knead for one minute. Cover lightly, set aside for at least one hour.

Pinch off egg sized pieces and roll into a ball. Let rest covered for 20 minutes.

Take each piece and flatten by rolling or patting from hand to hand. Make three or four holes in the bread keeping it from rising up in the middle and creating a hollow place when it fries.

The oil must be very hot. Cast iron skillets work best for frying bread. Put at least an inch of oil, melted shortening or lard and heat just to the smoking point. Most fry bread cooks add some used oil with the new oil to brown the bread nicely. Make sure all the rounds are prepared and put right into the oil to keep the oil from scorching. Cook until the brown color creeps up the side of the fry bread, then turn it over and cook a little longer to slightly browned.

Take fry bread out of frying pan and drain it on end, preferably over a rack that lets the oil drip off. Serve warm as Indian tacos or with something sweet such as honey, jam or fruit and cheese.

Author's Notes: Another form of fry bread is taking yeast bread dough and making individual flat rounds. Then put 3-4 holes in the center and fry like the recipe above. This product is lighter. An easy substitute is to use canned biscuits or thawed frozen yeast dough rolls, then flatten and fry.

GRIDDLE SCONES

Ingredients:

1 cup self rising flour
½ teaspoon baking soda
2 Tablespoons of soft butter
1 cup buttermilk
1 teaspoon golden syrup or treacle (mixture of half molasses and half pancake syrup)

Directions:

Cut or rub butter into the flour and add syrup, baking soda and buttermilk. Turn onto a floured surface and lightly handle the dough by patting it to ¾ inch thickness. Cut into rounds like a biscuit. Cook on greased griddle or heavy frying pan. The pan should be very hot. Brown on both sides. Serve freshly cooked scones with butter and jam for tea or breakfast.

Author's Notes: This is a handy recipe to have whenever you go camping or if you don't have access to an oven. I personally find that making these griddle scones the correct thickness to cook easily is more of an art than a science. It may take making this recipe more than once to gain the skill of knowing how long to cook one side before flipping it so the sides are evenly browned. I usually bake my scones and cut them into wedges, so in my opinion these round scones look more like an English muffin than a typical scone. Whatever you want to call them, they make a quick breakfast. Just about anything is good with butter and jam on it, and a wee cup of tea. Try them and see what you think.

PORRIDGE

Ingredients:

2 cups water
¼ teaspoon salt
¼ cup Oat-let fine oatmeal

Directions:

Soak overnight. In the morning simmer in a small pot, stirring often to keep them from sticking. Add more water if needed. Never let "them" boil. Porridge in the plural is referred to as them.

Author's Notes: I have eaten porridge all my life and suddenly discovered there is a real snobbery around the cooking and eating of this most simple food. I am told that you always use cold top cream, another name for half n half cream, poured carefully over the hot porridge. Then you must take your spoon and carefully go to the bottom of the bowl and bring the hot cereal up through the cold cream. Some claim no sweetening must ever be used other than fresh berries. Others claim only honey, or only butter and brown sugar, and on and on it goes. I say that variety is the spice of life and one day have it with cinnamon and the next with apples and the next with, well you get my meaning. To each his own. My personal snobbery is to make it from real oatmeal in a pot on the stove, not precooked in a plastic cup heated in the microwave. I can't explain it, it just seems wrong to me.

SALLY LUNN BREAD

Ingredients:

¾ cups of milk
2 eggs
6 Tablespoons of soft butter
1 package of dry yeast
3 cups of oat flour
1 ¼ teaspoon salt
¼ cup of warm potato water (drained off of boiled potatoes)
3 Tablespoons treacle also known as Golden Syrup (half molasses and half pancake syrup)

Directions:

Scald milk. Add yeast to lukewarm potato water. Test milk and make sure it is cooled to lukewarm. *Add water and yeast. Beat softened butter and sugar together. Add one egg at a time beating thoroughly after each egg. Stir in flour and salt, l cup of flour mixture into the butter and sugar and then stir in 1/3 of the yeast/milk mixture. Continue this process until all the ingredients are combined and batter is smooth. Cover the large mixing bowl with a clean towel and let batter rise for about 1 hour or until doubled in size. Stir the batter quickly to take out the air. Pour batter into a greased round casserole dish. Cover and let rise for 30 minutes or until double and then bake in a 350 degree Fahrenheit oven for 40-45 minutes. When the bread is done, take a butter knife to loosen the bread from the sides of the pan. Turn the bread upside down to remove the bread.

*How do you test milk to make sure it is lukewarm, you ask? Stick you finger into milk that has been heated and cooled for a while and drip that milk onto your wrist. If there is heat felt in the milk when it touches your wrist, it is still to hot. When it is not cool to your finger but the drop is not warm to your wrist, it is then lukewarm. It is similar to testing a baby's bottle of milk to make sure it is warm enough to drink but not so warm it will feel hot to the baby's mouth.

Author's Notes: According to legend Sally Lunn Bread came from the French phrase for sun-moon, soleil-lune (so-lay-LOON). Each loaf has a golden top (sun) and a white bottom (moon). Another story claims a pastry chef from Bath, England, named Solange Luyon sold these buns on the streets. Whatever the origin is of this unique bread, in Scotland the soleil-lune or Solange Luyon became "Sally Lunn", which is how the bread is known today. This bread does not stay fresh for more than a day so whatever is left from the day before is great for making into French toast. The loaf was usually made fresh daily and was referred to as "Our daily bread for which we give God thanks."

SCOTTISH OATCAKES

Ingredients:

8 ounces of pinhead oatmeal
2 Tablespoons of bacon drippings
½ teaspoon baking soda
½ cup hot water
Pinch of salt (1/8 teaspoon)
A little extra oatmeal for rolling cakes

Directions:

Use griddle or heavy frying pan. In a bowl add hot water and drippings or butter to dry ingredients and stir to make a soft paste. Sprinkle some oatmeal on a board to keep it from sticking. Form a dough into a round, then roll it with rolling pin as thinly as possible.

Cut dough into 4-6 pieces. If baking in oven bake at 375 degrees Fahrenheit for 15-20 minutes. To griddle bake until edges begin to curl. Turn over and cook other side. DO NOT let oatcakes brown; they should be a pale fawn color. Put on rack to cool. They are delicious with cheese.

Author's Notes: To test for the correct heat of the griddle sprinkle it with a little flour. If the flour browns at once it is too hot. It should take a few seconds to turn color and then it is the proper heat for cooking the oatcakes. Many of these bread or dessert recipes are prepared by using your senses rather than a strict procedure in a recipe. This is where art takes over the science of cooking or baking.

SPOON BREAD

Ingredients:

- 2 cups yellow corn meal
- 2 Tablespoons melted bacon grease
- 2 ½ cups boiling water
- 1 teaspoon baking soda
- 2 eggs-separated and at room temperature
- 1 ½ cups buttermilk
- 1 ½ teaspoons salt

Directions:

Add corn meal gradually to boiling water, stirring constantly. Let cool. Add bacon grease, salt, egg yolks, buttermilk and baking soda. Beat about 2 minutes and fold in stiffly beaten egg whites. Pour into well oiled baking dish or iron skillet and bake in a hot oven (425 degrees) for 40 minutes. Yield: 6 servings

Author's Notes: Spoon bread gets its name from using a spoon to put some of this corn bread type dish into the soup and then eat both soup and bread together. It is similar to how some people crush crackers up and put them in the soup. Or some prefer to put hot spoon bread in a bowl and cover it with cold milk, then eat it like a cereal. Part of the leavening for this bread is stiffly beaten egg whites. A trick you need to know about whipping egg whites is they will whip with more volume if they are at room temperature and not one drop of fat or egg yolk can be in the egg whites. If there is, they just will not whip up to create any volume. Adding egg whites to a recipe acts as part of the leavening so instead of the product being heavy and dense it will be lighter and have a better mouth feel.

DESSERTS

<u>CAKES</u>

<u>APPLE SPICE CAKE WITH BUTTERSCOTCH MERINGUE</u>-350 degrees Fahrenheit

Ingredients:

> 2 ½ cups all purpose flour
> 1 ½ teaspoons baking soda
> 1 ½ teaspoons of salt
> ¼ teaspoon baking powder
> 2 cups granulated sugar
> ¾ teaspoon ground cinnamon
> ½ teaspoon ground allspice
> ½ teaspoon ground cloves
> 1 ½ cups applesauce
> ½ cup of water
> ½ cup shortening
> 2 eggs-separated
> 1 cup raisins
> ½ cup chopped walnuts (also good with pecans or almonds)

Directions:

Beat all ingredients in large bowl on low speed, scraping bowl constantly for 30 seconds. Beat on high speed for 3 minutes. Pour into pans. Bake 35 to 45 minutes, or until inserted toothpick into center of cake come out clean.

<u>Author's Notes</u>: This is a delicious snack cake or breakfast coffee cake but for a fancier dessert add this butterscotch meringue.

Ingredients:

> 2 egg whites (see note from author)
> 1 Tablespoon lemon juice

1 cup packed brown sugar
½ cup of finely chopped nuts

Directions:

Just before cake is removed from the oven, beat egg whites until foamy. Beat sugar and lemon juice gradually into the egg whites until stiff. Carefully spread over hot cake. Sprinkle with nuts. Bake at 400 degree oven until brown, approximately 8-10 minutes. Cool slightly before cutting. If meringue sticks to knife, rinse in cold water and this should make it slice easier.

Author's Note: Have the egg whites at room temperature, they beat up fluffier and faster than when cold. Another secret is to use lemon juice or cream of tartar added to the raw egg whites. Remember this whenever making meringue for any pie, candies or other recipes requiring stiffly beaten egg whites. Use approximately 1/8 teaspoon of Cream of Tartar to every 2 egg whites.

MAMAW'S DEVIL'S FOOD CAKE WITH CHOCOLATE PECAN FROSTING

Ingredients:

2 cups granulated sugar
2 cups all purpose flour
½ cup butter
5 Tablespoon cocoa (not Dutch cocoa)
2 eggs
½ cup buttermilk+1 teaspoon baking soda
1 teaspoon vanilla
1 cup boiling water

Directions:

Beat sugar, butter, eggs and vanilla until creamy. Add flour and cocoa alternately with buttermilk with soda added to it. Lastly, stir in the hot water. Four into greased and floured long cake pan and bake for 25-30 minutes in a preheated 350 degree oven until done. Cool on rack and then frost with fudge frosting and top with chopped pecans. Garnish with fresh raspberries

FUDGE FROSTING

Ingredients:

8 ounces powdered sugar
4 Tablespoons melted butter
½ teaspoon real vanilla or bourbon
2 squares of chocolate, melted
1/3 cup of heavy whipping cream

Directions:

Sift sugar. Add all ingredients and beat until smooth and creamy. If too thin, add more powdered sugar until it achieves the desire consistency for cake frosting.

Author's Notes: I found this recipe and many others at the bottom of a box of photos that belonged to my grandparents. Most of the recipes were nothing more than a list of ingredients without directions about how to prepare them or at what temperature to bake them or for how long. Only cryptic clues were given such as: stir until it looks right, cook until done, season to taste and then no suggestions included as to what seasonings to use. Because this recipe was so old that the ink had faded and the paper was crispy brown, I went to my kitchen to experiment with what I thought I could understand from these recipes. Well to my surprise, what a treasure I discovered. This chocolate cake is delicious. It is made from scratch. And as the old joke goes, "It is very hard nowadays to find a box of scratch in the grocery store!"

LADY BALTIMORE CAKE WITH BUTTERCREAM FROSTING

Ingredients:

1 cup butter
2 cups granulated sugar
1 cup whole milk
½ teaspoon salt
4 teaspoons baking powder
3 ½ cups sifted cake flour
1 teaspoon real vanilla
6 egg whites+1/4 teaspoon Cream of Tartar

Directions:

Cream butter and sugar. Sift flour with baking powder and salt. Add alternately with milk to creamed butter and sugar. Add flavorings. Whip room temperature egg whites to stiff peaks. Fold egg whites into mixture. Pour into well oiled layer cake pans. Bake at 375 degrees Fahrenheit for 35 minutes or you see the cake pulling away from the sides of the pan and an inserted toothpick into the middle of the cake comes out clean.

BUTTERCREAM FROSTING

Ingredients:

½ cup shortening
½ cup butter
1 teaspoon almond extract
4 cups confectioner's sugar(also known as powdered sugar)
2 Tablespoons milk(add 2-4 Tablespoons if frosting a cake)

Directions:

Cream together shortening and butter. Add almond extract. Gradually add sugar, scraping sides well. Add milk between 2nd and 3rd cups of sugar. Beat until light and fluffy, approximately 5 minutes. Yields 3 cups.

Author's Notes: This is a modified recipe dated 1834. It was a common recipe for wedding cakes and this is what I thought was made for Matt and Adela's wedding cake.

PIES

<u>FLAKIEST PIE CRUST EVER!</u>

Ingredients:

> 2 ½ cups sifted all purpose flour
> 1 cup lard
> 1 teaspoon salt
> 1 eggs
> ¼ cup ice cold water
> 1 Tablespoon white vinegar

Directions:

Cut lard into the flour and salt. It should resemble course cornmeal. Beat egg with wire whip and combine with vinegar and ice cold water. Mix with flour, tossing lightly with a fork. If making a single pie crust for a cream pie bake at 450 degrees Fahrenheit for 8-10 minutes. Then place the rolled pie crust into a pie pan and prick it with a fork so the crust will not have bubbles in it or shrink too much in the pan.

<u>Author's Note:</u> This recipe was passed down to me from Susan Connor. Wherever you are Susan, thanks a million for this recipe. I've never had it fail to be the best pie crust and it has even won a few blue ribbons at the Alaska State Fair. You may use lard, shortening or butter. It's all good. This recipe is a 2 crust pie recipe.

PERFECT APPLE PIE

Ingredients:

2 crust pie dough
6 cups peeled sliced apples
¾ cup granulated sugar
2 Tablespoons all purpose flour
1 ½ teaspoon apple pie spice
¼ teaspoon salt
1 Tablespoon lemon juice
2 Tablespoons butter cut in pieces

Directions:

Preheat oven to 400 degrees Fahrenheit. Mix sliced apples with dry ingredients. Turn apple mixture into pastry lined pie plate, spread evenly. Scatter butter pieces over the top of apples. Fit top crust cover apples and press the edges together to seal and flute. Place in oven and bake until golden brown about 40-45 minute.

GIZZY'S BUTTERMILK PIE

Ingredients:

¼ cup all-purpose flour
½ cup melted butter, cooled
1 ½ cup granulated sugar
½ teaspoon salt
3 eggs
1 ½ teaspoons real vanilla
½ cup buttermilk
1-9 inch pie crust

Directions:

Melt butter. Mix sugar, salt and flour. Add eggs, buttermilk, vanilla to butter. Beat in dry ingredients. Beat thoroughly until smooth. Pour into prepared pie shell. Bake at 400 degrees Fahrenheit for 10 minutes then reduce heat to 350 degrees and bake for 40-45 minutes or until clean knife inserted into the middle of the pie comes out clean.

Author's Notes: A dear friend of mine who is a native Texan gave me permission to use her tried and true Buttermilk Pie recipe. It is the real thing!

PEACH COBBLER

Ingredients:

1 cup all-purpose flour
1 Tablespoon chilled butter
1/8 teaspoon salt
1 ½ cups sliced and pitted peaches
½ cup whole milk
1 Tablespoon baking powder
1/3 cup granulated sugar
½ teaspoon cinnamon

Directions:

Add all the dry ingredients except cinnamon and sugar. Cut butter into the flour mixture. Add milk. Turn onto lightly floured board and knead lightly. Place the peaches in a casserole dish. Sprinkle with cinnamon and sugar. Roll out the dough to cover the fruit. Cut slits to allow the steam to escape while baking. Bake at 450 degrees Fahrenheit for 30 minutes. While cobbler is in oven, boil an additional ¼ cup of sugar with ¼ cup of water. Add ¼ teaspoon of vanilla and during the last 10 minutes of baking, pour the syrup over the crust. Finish baking. Cool slightly then serve with ice cream or whipped cream.

Author's Notes: Use fresh or canned peaches or other fruit like blackberries. The Scots call blackberry cobbler, Bramble pie. All their pies have a crust on top of the fruit rather than a two crust pie, like American Apple Pie. Peach Cobbler, however, is the most favorite food of the fairies, so please do not leave any uneaten cobbler out on the kitchen counter overnight, it may all be gone by sunrise.

PEANUT BUTTER PIE

Ingredient:

2 egg slightly beaten
1 ½ cups of whole milk
¾ cups granulated sugar
5 Tablespoons flour
¼ teaspoon salt
½ teaspoon real vanilla
¾ cup Crunchy Peanut Butter
¼ teaspoon cinnamon
1/8 teaspoon ground cayenne pepper
1 9inch pie crust-baked
Whipped Cream to top pie
Chocolate Syrup

Directions:

Cook together eggs, milk, sugar, salt and flour until it thickens, about 7 to 10 minutes.

Remove from heat and add the vanilla, cinnamon, cayenne pepper and peanut butter. Pour into baked pastry crust. Cool pie. Serve with whipped cream drizzled with chocolate syrup.

PECAN TASSIES

Ingredients for Rich Crust:

> 3 ounces cream cheese
> 1 cup all purpose flour
> ½ cup butter

Directions:

Mix together and chill for 1 hour. After chilling, form into 2 dozen balls and press into muffin cups, lining the tins.

Ingredient for Pecan filling:

> ¾ cup brown sugar
> 1 teaspoon real vanilla
> 1 egg
> 1Tablespoon melted butter
> 2/3 cup of chopped pecans

Directions:

Beat together until smooth all ingredients, then add pecans. Pour into lined muffin tins. Bake at 325 degrees Fahrenheit for 25 minutes. Cool and remove from muffin tins. Yield: 2 dozen pecan teatime tassies.

COOKIES

SCOTCH SHORTBREAD

Ingredients:

2 cups sifted all-purpose flour
½ cup granulated sugar
1 cup butter
1 egg, unbeaten
½ teaspoon baking powder
grated rind of 1 lemon

Directions:

Sift flour, baking powder together. Cream butter thoroughly and add sugar slowly, creaming well. Stir in unbeaten egg and lemon rind. Add sifted dry ingredients to the mixture and work together on lightly floured board until smooth.

Divide dough in two parts and place each half on a greased 9 inch pie pan. Flatten with fingers and press into shape on bottom of pans. Mark into pie-shaped wedges with back of knife. Prick the dough with a fork. Bake in slow oven (300) degree Fahrenheit for 30 minutes. This dough makes 16 servings of shortbread, or may be cut into fancy shapes with cookie cutters if preferred.

Author's Notes:It is a Scotch custom to serve shortbread, fruitcake and a "wee drap" when friends drop in on holidays. Traditionally true shortbread is made with only three ingredient: flour, sugar and butter.

SNICKERDOODLE COOKIES

Ingredients:

    3 cups all purpose flour, spooned and leveled in cup
    1 teaspoon baking soda
    2 teaspoons cream of tartar
    ½ teaspoon salt
    1 cup butter, at room temperature
    ½ cup light brown sugar
    1 cup granulated sugar
    2 large eggs
    2 teaspoons real vanilla
    ½ cup sugar + 2 teaspoons cinnamon

Directions: (to roll the cookie dough in)

In a medium bowl combine flour, soda, cream of tartar and salt. With electric mixer beat butter and sugars until fluffy. Beat in eggs and vanilla. Discontinue using the mixer and stir in with wooden spoon, the dry ingredients until all is incorporated. Measure 1 level Tablespoon of dough per cookie ball and roll in cinnamon sugar, then place on cookie sheet, spacing 2 inches apart. Bake at 375 degrees Fahrenheit for 10 to 12 minutes. Cool slightly on cookie sheet, then remove to cool on wire rack. Yield: approximately 4 dozen cookies.

OATLET COOKIES

Ingredients:

1 cup softened butter
1 cup whole wheat flour
1 cup firmly packed brown sugar
¼ cup oat flour
½ cup granulated sugar
¼ cup finely chopped walnuts
4 eggs
1 teaspoon cinnamon
1 teaspoon real vanilla
1 teaspoon baking soda
½ teaspoon salt
3 cups uncooked oatlets-fine
¾ cups raisins or dried cherries
½ cup white chocolate chips
½ cup milk chocolate chips

Directions:

Heat oven to 350 degrees Fahrenheit. Beat butter and sugars together until creamy, add eggs and vanilla. Beat well. Combine all the dry ingredients and beat into the butter mixture. Stir in oat-lets, fruits and chocolates. Drop rounded tablespoon of dough onto cookie sheet. Bake for 10-12 minutes until golden brown. Cool and remove to wire rack.

Author's Notes: While cookies are still warm, have with ice cold milk or your favorite cup of tea. Yummy! There is a variation to this recipe that is rather wonderful, as well. Instead of adding fruit and chocolate, add an 8 ounce package of Heath English Toffee Bits or some of your homemade chocolate covered toffee that has been broken into small pieces. Roll the tablespoon of cookie dough in finely chopped pecans and then bake as the recipe directs. During the Holidays make a batch of each and no one will guess they are basically the same cookie recipe.

SWEETS

BUTTERSCOTCH HARD CANDY

Ingredients:

½ cup brown sugar
¼ cup butter
½ granulated sugar
2 teaspoons white vinegar
½ teaspoon real vanilla
few grains of salt

Directions:

Combine all ingredients except vanilla in a covered saucepan. Bring to a boil. Uncover and boil without stirring to soft crack stage (275-280 degrees Fahrenheit). Use candy thermometer for best results. Add vanilla. Do not stir. Pour quickly onto a well-buttered jelly roll pan or glass sheet cake pan, just as long as it has sides to it. Make a thin sheet. Cool slightly then mark the candy in small squares so it will break easily once it cools thoroughly. It should look like butterscotch colored glass.

CANDIED APPLE

Ingredients:

2 cups granulated sugar
¾ cups of water
½ cup light corn syrup
1 teaspoon red food coloring
1 teaspoon real vanilla
6 Granny Smith apples
6 skewers or Popsicle sticks
1 candy thermometer
Parchment paper/wax/or silicon mat
Vegetable non-stick spray
4 quart saucepan

Directions:

Line cookie sheet with parchment or other non-stick paper. Spray well with vegetable non- stick spray. Wash and dry apples. Insert skewers or sticks. Spray measuring cup with non-stick spray before adding corn syrup so it will slide out easier. Combine sugar, corn syrup, food coloring and vanilla in saucepan and blend. Cook on medium heat. Insert candy thermometer into mixture until it reaches the hard crack stage 290-310 degrees Fahrenheit. Do not leave mixture while cooking. The temperature jumps extremely hast and will quickly burn. When mixture reaches 300 degrees it is ready to dip the apples in. Dip twice and place on paper. If candy begins to harden in saucepan before you can dip all six apples, just place back on heat until the temperature reaches 300 degrees again. Let apple cool about 15-20 minutes. Serve. If you are not eating the apples right away then wrap them in cellophane bags or plastic wrap. Do not refrigerate or they will be very sticky.

Author's Notes: This is the recipe used for candied apples that are sold at the state fairs or carnivals. If you have ever had one you know they are difficult to eat. Also be forewarned not to attempt to make these candied apples if it is rainy or very humid because the candy will just run off the apple into a puddle.

WILD PLUM JELLY

Ingredients:

5 pounds of wild plums
1 ½ cups water
1 box Sure Gel pectin
7 ½ cups granulated sugar

Directions:

Wash and crush ripe tart plums. Do not peel or pit. Add water and simmer covered 10 minutes. . Place in jelly bag or cheese cloth and squeeze out juice. You will need 5 ½ cups of juice. Follow the directions inside the box of pectin for the best results.

Author's Notes: This is actually the same recipe for any kind of plum. I use wild sand plums. I think if you squeeze the juice out of the cheese cloth instead of letting it drip, the jelly has more flavor, however, if you feel like entering your plum jelly in the fair for judging for a prize, let it drip so the jelly will be clear and gem-like in color. That is what the judges are looking for in jellies.

ROSE PETAL AND ROSE HIP JELLY

Ingredients:

1 cup rose petals
1 cup rose hips
1 cup water
2 Tablespoons lemon juice
sugar

Directions:

Pack the rose petals and rose hips into the cup and press down tightly. Place in a saucepan and add water and lemon juice. Boil until the petals have a washed out color. Strain the liquid and measure it. Add ¾ as much sugar as you have liquid and boil. Boil rapidly for 10 minutes. Skim. Test on a small cold saucer to see if it will gel. Cook again until it passes the gel test. Pour into sterilized glass jars. Seal or cover with paraffin and store in a cool place.

Author's Notes: This is a delicate and beautiful addition to top baked goods or put into a hot cup of tea.

HOMEMADE ENGLISH TOFFEE CANDY

Ingredients:

2 cups + 1 Tablespoon softened butter (divided)
2 cups granulated sugar
1 Tablespoon corn syrup
¼ teaspoon salt
1 cup milk chocolate chips
1 cup finely chopped pecans

Directions:

Grease a 15 inch X 10 inch X 1 inch pan with 1Tablespoon of butter. In a large heavy saucepan melt the 2 cups of butter. Add sugar, corn syrup and salt. Cook and stir over medium heat until candy thermometer reaches 295 degrees (hard-crack stage). Quickly pour into prepared greased pan. Let stand at room temperature for1 hour. In double boiler or microwave, melt the chocolate chips and spread over toffee. Sprinkle pecans over the melted chocolate. Let cool. This can be broken into bit size pieces and stored in an air tight container.

Author's Notes: This candy makes great gifts at Christmas time.

AUNT BILL'S BROWN CANDY

Ingredients:

6 cups granulated sugar
2 cups heavy whipping cream
¼ pound of butter
¼ teaspoon saleratus (baking soda)
1 teaspoon vanilla
2 cups chopped pecans

Directions:

Pour two cups of sugar in an iron skillet and slowly heat to brown the sugar without burning it. Add cream and the rest of the sugar and bring to a boil. Cook until it forms a firm ball, whenever a small drop is tested in cold water. Remove from fire and add baking soda. Stir well then add butter. Let stand 10 minutes then add vanilla and chopped nuts. Beat until creamy. Pour into buttered dish and mark into squares, then cut when cooled.

Author's Notes: Important note is do not attempt to make this candy on a rainy day or whenever there is high humidity because it will never set up like fudge. Do not have any water on your utensils when you make this recipe or the sugar will crystallize and this confectioner is to feel very smooth and creamy in the mouth. This is a delicate confection to make but it is worth all the time and energy you put into its preparation. With all that said, are you ready to make some awesome candy? **Fun fact to know:** In many older recipes there is a term Saleratus. It is the same sodium bicarbonate that is now referred to as baking soda.

MEATS AND OTHER HIGH PROTEIN FOODS

ARENUMI'S STEW

Ingredients:

3 strips of bacon (save the bacon drippings)
3 large carrots or parsnips
2 pounds cubed beef (dredged in flour)
1 large onion, chopped
2 medium summer squash (sliced)
1 cup corn
6 pods of okra
salt and pepper to taste
½ teaspoon powdered sage
water to almost cover ingredients

Directions:

Fry bacon. Dredge cubed beef in flour seasoned with sage, salt and pepper. Brown the meat and chopped onions in the bacon drippings. Add carrots, okra and corn. Cover with water. Simmer on low heat for about 45 minutes. Add sliced summer squash and continue to simmer for another 15 minutes until squash is tender but not mushy.

Author's Notes: Dredging meat in flour just means to cover lightly with flour. When this is done and fried in hot grease or oil, it browns nicely which in turn make the stew or soup more appetizing to look at when you are eating it. It also helps to thicken the juices added to the recipe for a better texture and mouth feel. In this recipe the okra pods also help to thicken the juices and transform it into a delicious broth. Whenever the onions are browned with the floured meat, this serves to caramelize the sugars naturally found in the onions. This produces a distinct savory flavor that is totally different from the taste of fresh raw onions. Boiled meat and stewed meat are two different tastes.

People all over the world have made their diet from what was naturally available in their living area. The foods were made as healthy, tasty and convenient as possible. The basics for stew are mainly pieces of meat or beans and some root or starchy vegetables with liquid that is cooked long enough to thicken. Usually stew is eaten with a spoon but it is commonly accompanied by some sort of bread in which to soak up some of the broth. Use your own imagination and create a warm, savory and filling stew sopped up with delicious fry bread.

BBQ BRISKET

Ingredients:

4-5 pound beef brisket
2 teaspoons liquid smoke
2 teaspoons onion salt
2 teaspoons garlic salt
2 teaspoons celery salt
2 teaspoons wine vinegar
2 teaspoons Worcestershire sauce

Directions:

Rub liquid smoke on meat. Mix all ingredients and marinate meat over night in refrigerate. Grill outside or bake in oven to the doneness desired.

CROWDIE CHEESE (ALSO KNOWN AS COTTAGE CHEESE)

Ingredient:

4 rennet tablets
2 quarts of whole milk
4 teaspoons water or just used 4 teaspoons liquid rennet
4 Tablespoons of heavy cream
½ teaspoon of salt

Directions:

In a small bowl dissolve rennet tablets in the water. If you are using the liquid rennet omit this part of the directions. Slowly heat milk in an enamel or stainless steel saucepan until it reaches 98-100 degrees Fahrenheit on a candy thermometer or until a drop sprinkled on the wrist feels neither warm or cool. Remove from heat and stir in the rennet. In 5 to 20 minutes curds of cheese will form surrounded by the watery liquid called whey. Pour the contents of the pan into a sieve lined with double thickness cheese cloth and set over a bowl to drip. Let the cheese drip undisturbed for 1 ½ hours, then discard the whey and transfer the curds to a cooled bowl. (Place in refrigerator about an hour before needed. With a fork stir in salt and cream and mash the curds against the sides of the bowl until smooth. It is now ready to eat.

Author's Notes:This may be made with goat's milk and it tastes like feta cheese. This may be used in place of ricotta cheese in Italian dishes. Great with sliced tomatoes or fruit.

OLD FASHIONED SOUTHERN FRIED CHICKEN

Ingredients:

1 fryer chicken cut up
2 cups buttermilk
1 beaten egg
3 cups flour
2 teaspoons salt
1 teaspoon black pepper
2 Tablespoons dry poultry seasoning
Fat for deep fat frying

Directions:

Cut and wash chicken. Set up two large bowls, one with buttermilk and beaten egg in it and the other with flour with salt, pepper and poultry seasoning. Dip chicken first in flour then in buttermilk/egg wash, then back into flour. Make sure all the chicken is breaded before frying begins. To test the temperature of the oil drop a crumb of flour/buttermilk coating into the heated oil and when it bubbles up and fries, it is ready to add the chicken. Depending on the size of your frying pan or machine, you may have to fry the chicken in batches. Do not overcrowd the chicken so each piece will cook evenly and thoroughly. When you can see the edges of the chicken browning, turn and brown the other side. Partially cover with a lid for 10 minutes, then remove lid so the chicken will remain crispy. Stick a fork into the meat to see if it is fully cooked. If bloody water emerges, cook longer, you may even want to turn it again to cook longer on the other side as well. Drain on paper towel and place in 200 degree Fahrenheit oven to keep warm while you begin frying the next batch if you were unable to fry all the pieces at one time.

Author's Notes: Remember with all fried foods, the oil must be at the proper temperature because if it is too hot it will burn the breading and not fully cook the food, or if it is not hot enough, then the breading will absorb the oil and it will be greasy and not crispy. There was never a recipe for this until now. I just watched my Mamaw's fry chicken this way and this is the way I still fry chicken. When I worked at a restaurant during my college days, I prepared fried chicken this way and they liked it. Thanks you, Mamaw for your good Southern fried chicken. I'm offering this recipe for you to try and I hope you like it too. Some people have deep fat fryers which makes it very easy. I just use an old iron skillet. Also, rather than rolling the chicken pieces in flour, I put the flour in a plastic bag and shake the flour onto the milk coated chicken. This makes it less messy to prepare and much easier to clean up once the frying is completed.

CHICKEN CREAM GRAVY

Directions:

If you fried the chicken in a skillet, use the same skillet to make the cream gravy. Pour off all but about 4 Tablespoons of fat. Leave the brown crumbs that cooked off the chicken while it was frying. Heat this fat until it boiling hot. Sprinkle 1 heaping tablespoon of flour over the hot fat. It should bubble and begin to brown. Stir constantly so it will not burn. When it is nicely brown, add 1 cup of milk and/or more milk or water as it thickens so it will stay creamy. Remove from heat because it will continue to thicken. Leftover gravy may be reheated and thinned down with a little bit of water or chicken broth.

Author's Notes: Some people make cream gravy and it looks more like a white sauce. Good Southern cream gravy must have a cooked rue before the milk and or water is added. Instead of salt, for my cream gravy, I sprinkle a pinch of chicken bouillon and stir it in with the milk/water. Leftover gravy is great for breakfast with hot biscuits, eggs, hash browns or cottage fried potatoes and some sort of breakfast meat. OK, I'm hungry now.

DEVILED EGGS

Ingredients:

6 hard cooked eggs
Mayonnaise
salt and pepper
½ teaspoon capers, minced
½ sweet relish
½ teaspoon onion, minced
Paprika to garnish the top of the egg

Directions:

Cut peeled egg in halves lengthwise. Remove yolk. Mash and moisten egg yolk with mayonnaise until creamy. Add all the other ingredients except paprika. Blend until light and fluffy. Fill center of egg whites with egg yolk mixture. Garnish with paprika on top. Serve chilled.

FRIED FISH AND HUSH PUPPIES

Directions:

There are all kinds of ways to cook fish, but the old fashioned way was either to boil it to make a fish stew or chowder; another way was to fry it. This was simple: catch it, gut it, cut it into portion sizes, roll it in cornmeal seasoned with salt and pepper and fry it in whatever fat was available.

Ingredients for hush puppies:

2 cups cornmeal
1 egg
1 cup buttermilk
1 teaspoon salt
1 Tablespoon flour
½ teaspoon baking soda
1 Tablespoon finely chopped onion
1 teaspoon baking powder

Directions:

Mix all dry ingredients together. Add onion, buttermilk and beaten egg. Drop by tablespoonful into skillet in which fish has been fried. Fry to a golden brown and drain on paper towel. The hush puppies will float to the surface if fried in a deep fat frier or deep skillet.

Author's Notes: Legend has it that the cornmeal left from breading the fish would be used to make a type of fry bread called hush puppies. It was because the dogs would be hungry whenever they smelled fish cooking and would begin to howl for food. These little balls of fried cornmeal were tossed to the dogs to stop their howling. The cook would yell, "Hush Puppies!" Well, I don't know if it's true but it makes for a cute story.

FROG LEGS*

Directions:

Remove the legs off the frog, skin them and wash under cold running water. Heat oil or grease in a heavy skillet. Bend the frog leg to break and loosen the knee joint. Make an egg wash as if frying chicken. Dip in egg/milk wash and then in seasoned flour. Fry until they are brown and the meat is pulling away from the bone.

*CAUTION: Do not fry in too hot of grease because there is water trapped within the legs of the frog that will come out during cooking and cause the grease to pop and spatter. Also, the meat needs to be tender and completely cooked.

Author's Notes: There is a proper way to dispose of the parts of the frog not eaten. Gather up the frog bodies, thank them for their tasty legs and then return them to the pond or water where you caught them. It is the ancient respectful way to treat the life that sustains your life.

FRIED HAM WITH RED-EYE GRAVY

Directions:

Have a frying pan very hot so the precooked smoked ham slices will quickly brown on both sides. Lower the heat and continue to cook until warmed thoroughly. The time for cooking will depend on how thick you cut the ham slices. Remove from pan. You will want some of the ham juice browned on the skillet. If there is not enough fat on the meat to make enough gravy, add some lard or oil (not butter) to the frying pan. When done, pour the grease into a bowl, set the pan back on the burner of the stove and heat. Add about ½ cup of water to the pan and bring to a boil, which should remove the brown ham juice from the bottom of the skillet. Add back to the skillet the grease. Have homemade biscuits ready and pour some of the gravy over them and eat with the ham.

Author's Notes: My daddy told me "Real" red-eye gravy always has coffee in it, not just water. I must warn you, this is an acquired taste.

INDIAN AND PIONEER JERKY (DRIED MEAT)

Outdoor method:

Build a small campfire by using small limbs of green hardwood such as maple, aspen or alder. Make a drying rack over the fire (3 or 4 feet above the fire) of chicken wire or small limbs of green wood. Let the fire burn down to coals then add green wood and some leaves to create smoke. To prepare meat use the best portions of muscle meat from beef, deer, bison, moose, caribou or elk. Cut away all the fat lengthwise of the grain of meat. Cut into strips as long as possible, but not more than 1-inch wide and thick. It is tastier if the meat is salted and peppered before drying. Lay the well-seasoned strips of meat across the rack leaving a small space between each piece of meat so smoke can surround the pieces during the drying time. Keep smoke continuously under the meat for 10 to 15 hours. The meat is dry when it turns black or dark brown in color and becomes brittle. Store in some container to avoid getting moisture in it.

Oven Dried method: The meat is prepared as above. Place the strips of meat on the wire rack within the oven. Dry at 150-200 degrees Fahrenheit for about 25 hours. Place these strips of meat in an old pillowcase and hang in a dry place before storing in a tight container. The meat should keep indefinitely if kept dry. Stew is excellent made from dried jerky.

Author's Notes: Over 120 years ago, jerky was carried in the pocket or jacket of a person who was traveling or hunting. Now it is sold in every convenience store as a snack food. When making your own I will caution you about a few things to keep in mind. Many people who suffer from plant allergies may be sensitive to cottonwood or birch wood smoke. Also, pork and bear meat have too much fat within the muscle meat, so if used the meat will not store well and become rancid quickly.

PEMMICAN

Directions:

Pemmican is best when made from bison jerky although it can be made from any kind of wild game except greasy meat like pig, porcupine or bear. Pound or grind the dried jerky. Obtain marrow fat by cracking the animal bones then boil the bones. Cool, skim off the fat and use the broth for a soup base. To about one pound of ground jerky add 1 cup of ground raisins or other dried fruit. Add 1 cup of marrow fat. Mix all ingredients together in a shallow pan or stuff into muslin bags to cool. Break the cooled pemmican into pieces and store in cloth or paper bags. Hang in a cool dry place. This will keep indefinitely and is a life saver if stranded in the wilderness.

Author's Notes: I first learned about this strange recipe while I worked at Comanche Memorial Hospital in Lawton, Oklahoma. I was re-acquainted with it in ground school when I was getting my flight training. My instructor told me he always kept some pemmican in the emergency bag in his airplane. Comanche and other Plains Indians ate this high protein, high fat and moderate carbohydrate food to keep from suffering malnutrition during long winter months whenever hunting was sparse. This does not have the texture of fresh meat but rather similar in texture to ground nuts. It is surprisingly quite palatable; savory/sweet.

ROASTED PHEASANT

Directions:

Pheasant is a game bird and the female has the most fat content, therefore is tastier than the male. To help keep the meat moist and flavorful, place a pat or two of butter between the breast skin and the breast meat. Then drape strips of lean bacon over the entire body of the pheasant. To season the bird use any poultry seasoning such as a few twigs of rosemary, fresh thyme and sage within the cavity of the bird. Roast at 350 degrees Fahrenheit the same as you would a small domestic chicken. Do not over-cook or the meat will be dry and stringy. When the pheasant meat is pulling away from the joint on the drum stick that was cut away from the foot, remove from oven and take off the strips of bacon. Return to oven to brown for approximately 10-15 minutes. This meat is complimented with some sort of fruit sauce, such as cranberry or wild plum sauce.

Author's Notes: Duck, prairie chicken, goose and other wild fowl may be roasted like pheasant. Other wild game such as venison, bison, moose, caribou, deer, or elk may be cooked like beef. Fatter meats such as wild pig or bear need to be cooked to well done. The taste of the meat depends on what the animal has been feeding upon and how merciful the hunter was with the killing of the animal. My grandfather impressed upon me to be a darn good shot if I ever wanted to go hunting. He told me never shoot and just wound the animal because then it has to be chased down and this causes the animal to suffer. More adrenaline is pumped into the animal as it runs and this produces a stronger flavor. When the hunter field dresses the animal (gutting and removing the hide) the hunter must be skilled so the animals urine or bile will not touch the muscles of the animal. Hang the carcass so it can bleed out. Cover with game cloth so air may circulate through to the meat and also keep the flies off of it. Bleed all meats, foul or red meat. Be clean and keep the meat clean. If you are uncertain how to butcher, have it professionally done or learn how. There's a mountain of information on this subject if you are interested. I think our next generation needs to add this information to their "need to know" skills in life.

QUAIL

Directions:

Quails do not have to be plucked. Pull the skin off, remove head, feet and entrails. Rub the inside and outside of bird with butter, salt and pepper. Place in a roasting pan and cover. Bake in 350 degree Fahrenheit oven until tender when pricked with a knife. When done, uncover and return to oven to brown for about 10 minutes. Quail can be cut into pieces and also cooked like chicken or Rock Game Cornish Hen. Roll in seasoned flour and fry in hot oil. Fry to brown on both sides and then reduce heat, cover, and slowly cook so that it is "good and done", as we say in Oklahoma.

RABBIT

Directions:

Remove the pelt. Cut the young rabbit into sections. Salt and pepper and roll in flour and fry in hot lard. Remove rabbit and all but 3 Tablespoons if lard. Add 2 Tablespoon of flour, stirring constantly to brown the flour but not let it burn. Add equal amounts of milk and water and cook until the gravy thickens. Serve rabbit with hot biscuits and the cream gravy. Salt if needed. If the rabbit is old, parboil so it will be tender and then fry as instructions for young rabbit.

Author's Notes: Of course all meat can be roasted but with rabbit it is tougher to chew so braise, fried or boiled seems to make for a more desirable meal of rabbit. There is an old tale about rabbits loving their fur. The moral of this story is if you use their pelts in addition to their meat, you will be blessed and the rabbits will be happy to have been a blessing.

SAUSAGE: BLACK AND WHITE PUDDING

Ingredients:

4 cups fresh pig blood
2 ½ teaspoons salt
1 ½ cups pinhead (steel-cut) oatmeal
2 cups finely diced pork fat
l large onion, finely chopped
1 cup milk
1 ½ teaspoons black pepper
1 teaspoon ground allspice

Directions:

Preheat oven to 325 degrees Fahrenheit and grease 2 glass loaf pans. If you don't have glass loaf pans, line metal pans with parchment to keep the blood sausage from reacting with the metal creating an off flavor. Stir 1 teaspoon of salt into the blood. Bring 2 ½ cups water to a boil and stir in the oats. Simmer, stirring occasionally, for 15 minutes, just until tender but not mushy.

Pour blood through a fine sieve into a large bowl to remove any lumps. Stir in fat, onion, milk, pepper, allspice and remaining 1 ½ teaspoon of salt. Add the cooked oats and mix to combine. Divide the mixture between the loaf pans, cover with foil and bake for 1 hour, until firm. Cool completely. Seal in plastic wrap and wither freeze for extended use or store in refrigerator for up to a week. To serve cut a slice about ½ inch thick off the loaf. Fry in butter or oil until the edges are slightly crisped and brown. To make white pudding, use the same recipe except use 4 cups of finely chopped cooked pork instead of blood.

Author's Notes: While visiting Scotland, Ireland and Germany we tasted each countries type of blood sausage. All over the world people have been eating blood sausage, but if you did not grow up with it as part of your diet, I shall warn you it is an acquired taste. Also, all of the ones we tried were prepared by stuffing the ingredients into sausage casing, then cooked. A traditional breakfast in Scotland and Ireland include Black and White Pudding with eggs and an assortment of breakfast breads with jams, jellies or lemon curd. So many dishes are referred to as pudding. The American definition of pudding is a sweet smooth milk-based dish eaten with a spoon for snack or dessert. In Britain, it can be steamed cake, sausage or other foods.

TURKEY AND STUFFING OR DRESSING

Directions for selecting a turkey

Pick the weight of a turkey that will provide for the number of people you are preparing to serve during the Holidays. Refer to a chart in a cookbook or other reliable source, such as Google or Pinterest for cooking times and poundage per person. The one I use states: 8-10 pound turkey bake at 325 degrees, 20 minutes per pound; 18-20 pounds, 14 minutes per pound. The important thing is to make sure the internal temperature is 175 degrees Fahrenheit when you consider it done. I suggest a fresh turkey, void of hormones, that has been fed organic food and allowed to free-range instead of being caged for life. Stuffing a turkey or baking the stuffing recipe outside the bird, which is called **dressing**, will depends on your taste. The reason seasoned bread crumbs were stuffed inside the cavity of the bird was to add flavor to them from the juices dripping from the bird while being roasted. One of the main reasons some prefer dressing to stuffing is that some are not confident that the internal temperature of the bird will rise high enough to keep bacteria from growing in the bread crumbs inside the bird. My daddy always cooked the Holiday meals and he preferred dressing to stuffing, but this recipe may be used for stuffing the turkey or any type of fowl.

Ingredients for Jim Welty's Cornmeal Dressing

2 cups or more Turkey broth from roasted turkey
½ cup butter, melted
2 small chopped onions
2 beaten eggs
1 Tablespoon Poultry seasoning
¾ cup diced celery
3 cups soft buttermilk biscuit crumbled
Chopped cooked giblets
1 cup cornbread crumbled
Salt and pepper to taste

Directions:

   Cook giblets in water for meat and broth to be used in the dressing. Saute celery and onions in butter. Bake biscuits and cornbread in advance and crumble up enough to measure out what the recipe requires. Place in a large bowl and add poultry dressing and the cooked celery and onions and chopped giblets. Add beaten eggs and enough turkey broth to moisten the mixture. Place in buttered casserole dish and bake at 350 degrees Fahrenheit for 35-40 minutes. Serve with the sliced turkey, mashed potatoes and turkey gravy.

SOUPS

SCOTTISH COCKALEEKIE SOUP

Ingredients:

5 ½ to 6 pounds of stewing chicken
5 quarts of water
6 or 7 large leeks including 2 inch green leafy portion
½ cup barley
(about 8 cups chopped)
1 Tablespoon salt
2 Tablespoon finely chopped parsley

Directions:

Wash and cut up chicken. Stew in 5 quarts of water until chicken is falling off the bones. Remove meat from broth. Cool and remove skin and bones and cut into smaller pieces of meat for the soup. Add chicken back to the broth in addition to the leeks and barley. Reduce the heat and simmer on low for about 3 hours. Add salt. Serve sprinkled with parsley. Yield: 4 to 5 quarts.

Author's Notes" Leeks have a milder flavor than onions, unless you use sweet onions such as Maui or Vidalia. Leeks are more expensive so I use half leeks and half onions. Leeks need to be thoroughly washed to remove any hidden pockets of sand or mud. Cut diagonally into ½ inch slices.

SCOTCH BROTH

Ingredients:

2 pounds lamb neck or shoulder with bones
1 cup finely chopped leeks
2 quarts of water
½ cup chopped celery
2 Tablespoons barley
½ cup green peas
1 Tablespoon finely chopped parsley
Small piece shredded cabbage
½ cup thinly sliced carrot or parsnip
½ cup chopped turnip

Directions:

Brown lamb in a small amount of fat. Place in a heavy 4 to 6 quart dutch oven or saucepan. Add water and bring to a boil. Add barley and simmer for 1 hour or until meat pulls away from the bone. Add all the vegetables except parsley and lower the heat and cook until vegetables are tender. Serve in bowls with parsley and dulce sprinkled over the soup. The dulce is optional. It is a salty seaweed that is dried and used instead of regular salt.

Author's Notes: This hearty soup is great on a misty moisty day when cloudy is the weather! Serve with oatcakes and Crowdie cheese and your favorite cup of tea. Scotch Broth is somewhat like Mom's meatloaf. Every Mom makes it just a little different and if the truth be known, Moms make use of what they have available to feed their families. Basically, this is a bone broth with or without meat and what ever vegetables are on hand. Another name for this soup is Barley Broth, but potatoes or rice can easy replace the barley. I tell you this because this recipe is just a suggestion of ingredients. If you feed it to someone who claims this is not the REAL Scotch Broth, smile sweetly at them and then ask them for their recipe.

VEGETABLE DISHES

FRESH GREEN BEANS WITH HAM HOCK AND NEW POTATOES

Ingredients:

½ pound ham hocks
3-4 pounds fresh green beans
chicken broth to cover beans
1 teaspoon ground turmeric
2-3 new potatoes per person
1 Tablespoon minced garlic

Directions:

Wash and snip the ends off of the green beans. Use a large cooking pot and cover the beans and ham hock with chicken broth and seasonings. Cover and simmer for about an hour. Add potatoes and cook until tender when tested with a paring knife.

Author's Notes: This recipe will serve about 6 to 8 adults as a side dish. Green beans with ham hocks made in a big batch freezes well and is always popular year around. This dish goes well with fried chicken, sliced tomatoes, Sally Lunn bread and pickles. Forget all that, this dish goes well with everything or all by itself!

SCOTTISH BAKED BEANS

Ingredients:

1 pound small cleaned white dry beans
½ cup diced onion
¼ cup treacle or molasses
1 ½ teaspoon salt
1 teaspoon dry mustard
¼ cup brown sugar
½ teaspoon fresh ground pepper
¼ cup apple cider vinegar
1 cup salt pork or bacon
Dash of pepper sauce

Directions:

Sort and wash the beans. Add 10 cups of hot water in a cooking pot and heat to boiling for 2-3 minutes. Remove from heat and let stand at least 4 hours. Drain off the soaking water. Transfer beans to a large casserole dish. Combine dry ingredients and mix into beans. Stir in onion, molasses or treacle, brown sugar, vinegar and bacon. Pour a quart of boiling water on top of the beans. Cover with lid and bake at 300 degrees Fahrenheit for 6 hours. Check periodically and add boiling water if needed during cooking.

Author's Notes: This recipe was copied from an old recipe written on paper that was yellowed with age and crumbing on the edges. I baked these beans as directed and found they took a bit too much watching for me on my busy day. So I modified this recipe by soaking the beans overnight, pouring the soak water off and putting them into my crock pot with all the ingredients. Then I cooked them all day. They were perfectly done for supper. Since this recipe was written per-crock pot days, it is handy to have if you want to cook beans in the oven My grandmother cooked beans on wash day so she could scrub the clothes, check the beans, hang out the clothes, check the beans, take in the dried clothes, check the beans, sprinkle the clothes, take out the cooked beans for supper. That worked for her. But my method leaves me the entire day to work on laundry and other household chores, or write novels.

PICKLED BEETS

Ingredients:

10 pounds of fresh cleaned beets
2 cups granulated sugar
1Tablespoon pickling salt (no iodized salt)
1 quart (4 cups) white vinegar
¼ cup whole cloves
2 cups liquid from cooked beets

Directions:

In large pot cover 10 pounds of clean beets with water. Cook until tender. Drain all but 2 cups of water off the beets. Cool. Peel and slice or cube cooked beets and pack in sterilized canning jars.. Divide evenly the whole cloves in the jars filled with beets. In a smaller saucepan bring to boil sugar, salt, vinegar, and reserved beet liquid. Pour hot liquid over beets and cover with sterilized canning lids. Process 10 minutes in a hot water bath. Remove, cool and check lids to assure the lids have sealed to the jars. May be eaten immediately.

Author's Notes: As with all canning, review canning methods before you start. Make sure you use the manufacturer's directions and keep the work area very clean from anything that may contaminate the product being canned. This is a recipe for a large amount that may easily be cut into half, if desired.

BREAD AND BUTTER PICKLES

Ingredients:

12 large cucumbers
12 large sweet onions
2 cups white vinegar
1 ½ cups granulated sugar
1 teaspoon dry mustard
1 teaspoon powdered turmeric
1 teaspoon celery seed
1 teaspoon dry ginger
1 teaspoon powdered alum

Directions for bread and butter pickles:

Peel cucumbers and onions, slice and put into brine for 2 hours (brine is ¼ cup non-iodized salt, 4 cups of iced water and alum). Drain. Mix vinegar, sugar and spices in large cooking pot and bring to boil. Add cucumbers and onions. Cook 5 minutes then pack in hot freshly wash canning jars. Ladle some of the hot liquid to cover the pickles. Seal and store in a cool dark place for about 4 weeks before opening the jar.

Author's Notes: Whenever you have your jelly making jars and pots out at the end of summer, go ahead and try your hand at pickle making. There are all kinds of recipes and kits to use but this is an old family favorite. My mother would make a batch and let the jars set until she opened the first jar of the season for Thanksgiving dinner.

CHOW-CHOW RELISH

Ingredients:

1/4 Peck or ½ gallon green tomatoes
7 onions
½ Tablespoon grated horseradish
1 tablespoon turmeric
½ tablespoon celery seed
1 large cabbage
12 cucumbers
½ tablespoon black pepper
2 teaspoons ground cinnamon

Directions:

Chop onions, green tomatoes, cucumbers and cabbage into very small pieces. Pack them in a crock or glass bowl with salt slightly sprinkled over all the vegetables, cover and place them in the refrigerator over night. In the morning pour off the brine liquid that formed overnight from the chopped vegetables. Mix half white vinegar and water to cover the vegetables and refrigerate for two days. Drain the vinegar water off. Mix the spices and stir into the vegetables. Boil 4 cups of white vinegar with 3 pounds of granulated sugar. Pour over vegetables while hot. Seal in jars. It will be ready to eat in two weeks. Store in sealed jars in a cool place away from sunlight. Use in place of sweet or dill relish on hot dogs, hamburgers, meat salads or potato salad. Mix with equal part of mayonnaise and ketchup for a delicious Thousand Island dressing for green salads or Reuben sandwiches.

ROASTING EARS OR CORN ON THE COB

Ingredients:

Enough corn so each person can have two whole corns on the cob.

Directions:

Pull the corn leaves away from the ear to remove the silk but do not remove the leaves. Wrap a strip of bacon around the corn. Pull up the leaves to cover over the bacon. Roast on a BBQ grill or in a 400 degree Fahrenheit oven for 20-25 minutes. Remove leaves and bacon. Serve. There is not need for butter or salt.

FRIED OKRA

Ingredients:

Fresh tender okra pods
½ cornmeal and 1/2 flour mixture
beaten egg
Oil for frying-Peanut oil is best

Directions:

Wash the fresh okra and slice into a bowl of beaten egg. Depending on how much okra you wish to fry, you may have to add more beaten eggs, one at a time, so all the okra will be coated. Then place some cornmeal and flour into a bowl and coat the egged okra in the cornmeal/flour mixture. Drop into hot oil and fry until crispy brown. Drain on paper. Salt and serve. The breading may stay on better when fried if after breading the okra it is frozen on a cookie sheet, then fried while frozen.

Author's Notes: Fried Okra just happens to be my comfort food. It can also be stewed or put into soups as a thickener. I am still shocked and amazed how many people alive today do not know what okra is!?! This is my small attempt to enlighten those poor souls to the wonderfully delicious seed pod known as okra. Will you join with me to accomplish my mission? Depending on who you ask the word "Okra" is from the Angolan, African, word ngombo which means okra or the Nigerian Igbo language Okuru meaning sticky seed pod or the Choctaw Native American word Kombo which all mean okra that is the main ingredients in preparing the Creole Louisiana dish, Gumbo. Okra is also used as an herbal medicine for intestinal discomfort. Okra is also tasty whenever it is pickled. The okra plant grows well in hot climates. Now you know everything I know about OKRA.

MINA'S PICKLED OKRA

Ingredients:

    4 cups white vinegar
    4 cups of water
    ½ cup of salt
    24 diced red peppers
    12 large jalapeno pepper
    24 cloves garlic
    12 teaspoon dill seed
    Enough small okra pods to fill 12 pint jars

Directions:

Boil vinegar, water and salt. Pack okra into sterilized pint jars and add 1 jalapeno pepper, 1 teaspoon of dill seed, 2 diced red peppers and 2 cloves of garlic to each jar of okra. Pour boiling solution of salty vinegar water into the jars and seal. Wait at least 2 weeks before opening and eating the pickled okra.

GREEN PEA SALAD

Ingredients:

2 cups cooked small green peas, also known as English peas
½ cup diced cheddar cheese
2 hard cooked eggs
½ cup of relish or chow-chow
¼ cup chopped pimento
1 Tablespoon minced onion
¼ cup mayonnaise
Salt and pepper to taste

Directions:

Combine all ingredients. Chill until ready to serve.

Author's Notes: Whenever picking and shelling peas, place the smallest peas aside and cook them together. Sort out the larger one and cook them together because it stands to reason that the larger peas take longer to cook and if the smaller ones were among them they would become overcooked. Use the smaller peas to make this salad or to puree for babies to eat. If you do not use fresh peas, buy the smallest sized canned peas. Some cooks garnish this salad with little bacon bits. Did you hear that BACON LOVERS?

REAL MASHED POTATOES

Directions:

Count a medium sized potato for each adult served. Wash off the surface and peel if desired, it is not necessary. Cube and place into a saucepan with salted water that will barely cover the potatoes. Cook by simmering until tender. Avoid boiling hard since this will bring out the starch and cause the potatoes to have a gluey texture. Drain and save the potato water for soups or for dissolving the yeast when making wheat bread or rolls. In another pan warm some milk and butter. Add a small amount as you mash the potatoes. Keep adding the warm milk and butter until you achieve the texture you desire. By heating the milk and butter, it will help keep the potatoes warm as you serve them at the meal. These potatoes should be fluffy, not runny or dry. They should be stiff enough to hold their shape when gravy is poured over them.

Author's Notes: There are many varieties of potatoes. The best varieties used for mashing, baking and frying are mealy potatoes such as russet or purple potatoes. New potatoes, or what is commonly known as Irish red potatoes are called waxy potatoes and are best for soups, stews, hash browns or potato salad. Many things may be added for variety to this basic bland flavored food. Some suggestions are: bacon bits, sour cream, shredded cheese, green onion tops or chives, garlic-fresh or powdered. Flavor is enhanced when cooked in beef or chicken broth. This choice will depend upon the accompanying meat. Leftover mashed potatoes may be used for the next morning's breakfast by adding an egg to the potatoes and formed into a patty and fried. Leftover mashed potatoes are handy for making a quick cream of potato soup or fish chowder. I haven't yet exhausted the many uses of the average mashed potato. Use your imagination for additional recipe ideas. That is what our mothers and grandmothers have done for centuries in order to feed their hungry families and friends.

CHAPPIT TATTIES AND BASHED NEEPS ALSO KNOWN AS MASHED POTATOES WITH MASHED TURNIPS

There is no recipe for this dish. It is Scottish in origin and it is mainly cooking potatoes and turnips and mashing them together. Before serving, butter and parsley may be added as well as salt and pepper at the table for individual's liking. The reason I included this dish in the small cookbook in the appendix of 40 Days with Ruth is because this is a blend of two cultures. Potatoes are originally from the American continents and the turnip was brought over from Europe but is believed to have originated in middle to eastern Asia. It is part of the mustard family and is cultivated for its fleshy roots as well as the tender growing tops.

FRIED GREEN TOMATOES

Tomatoes and potatoes are from the nightshade family. Tomatoes are botanically a fruit but are prepared and eaten like vegetables. Other than Chow-Chow, this is another good use of green tomatoes. Take a large green tomato and cut crosswise in large slices. Dip each slice into beaten egg and then dip each into seasoned corn meal. Fry in hot lard or fresh bacon grease until brown on both sides. Serve hot.

Author's Notes: If I were a betting woman, I'd bet the origin of this dish was created by some dear farmer's wife who had a great number of green tomatoes left on the vine at first frost. Being of frugal Scottish decent, the idea came to her in an instant. "What shall I do with all these dang green tomatoes? I know, I'll make relish with them and what is left over I'll fry them and call them good," Well, so she did, and they are GOOD!

WATERMELON RIND PICKLES

Ingredients:

4 pounds watermelon rind
2 cups white vinegar
2 cups water
4 cups sugar
3 cinnamon sticks
1 teaspoon whole cloves
1 teaspoon whole allspice
1 lemon
Brine: ¼ cup salt and 4 cups of water

Directions:

Pare watermelon rind and remove skin and all of the pink flesh so only the white portion is left. Cut into bite size pieces. Weigh to make sure there is 4 pounds. Soak in brine overnight. In the morning drain and rinse the rind. Combine remaining ingredients and boil for 5 minutes. Add a few pieces of rind at a time and cook until rind is clear. Pack quickly into sterilized jars. Cover with boiling syrup and seal. Let jars set a few weeks before eating.

Author's Notes: I never cease to be amazed at some of the foods people, throughout the centuries, have chosen to eat. Who would think of pickling watermelon, cantaloupe, pumpkin or squash rind? But as you see, they did and still do. These pickles are a sweet tangy morsel that is very refreshing as a condiment with almost an y meal. Plus, the Scot within me receives a noble feeling about living without being wasteful.

Printed in the United States
By Bookmasters